Welcoming the Little Ones

Your Guide to a Faith-filled Parish Nursery

Beth Branigan McNamara
Gina Wright McKeever

Our Sunday Visitor Publishing Division
Our Sunday Visitor, Inc.
Huntington, Indiana 46750

Copyright © 1998 by Our Sunday Visitor Publishing Division, Our Sunday Visitor, Inc. ALL RIGHTS RESERVED.

International Standard Book Number: 0-87973-927-4

Library of Congress Catalog Card Number: 97-69274

Cover design and illustrations by Tyler Ottinger

Some illustrations are based on designs by Brenda Anderson

Printed in the United States of America

Contents

Foreword

On Sunday morning throughout the world, people gather to celebrate the Lord's Day. It is this day and the celebration we gather for that is at the heart of our lives as Christians. The Liturgy, or Celebration of the Eucharist, according to the Second Vatican Council, is the source and summit from which all our Christian activity flows. This goes for people who work professionally in church ministry, for ordinary people who minister with their time and talent, for individuals and families as they go about their lives during the week, for all God's people — young and old. This is the body of Christ, we people living and working, making the presence of Jesus Christ seen and felt.

At St. Pascal Baylon Parish in St. Paul, Minnesota, the Lord's Day is one of great celebration, thanksgiving, and formation. At the heart of our morning is the people gathering to break open God's Word and sharing in the Sacrament of the Body and Blood of the Lord. Jesus Christ becomes present for his sisters and brothers in order to share God's Love and Grace.

As part of this morning, time is also given to formation. Formation allows us to grow in our faith, taking what we have been taught from the Church and making it a part of our lives. This has been happening with our preschoolers through our adults. But now I am happy to see this can be a part of the lives of some of our little-est ones. This is now happening in our Sunday nursery.

Our Sunday nursery is not just a place to drop off our toddlers for baby-sitting, but a place where formation can begin. Even with very simple faith our little-est ones can know that this day — The Lord's Day — is special for them too. They come and learn and meet Jesus as their parents experience Jesus at Mass. I hope your parish community and little ones will enjoy this nursery program as much as ours are. I am grateful to Beth McNamara and Gina McKeever for writing this program and helping our parish nurseries become places of faith sharing and catechesis, formation at some of our simplest levels.

Not too long ago these children were plunged in the waters of baptism. We as members of the Body of Christ pledge that we will help the parents of these children in their duty to share the faith of the Church. We are never too young to learn about Jesus and this nursery program gives us a new opportunity to share in the catechesis and faith formation of these little ones.

Father Thomas Brioschi, Pastor
The Church of St. Pascal Baylon
St. Paul, Minnesota
January 1998

Introduction
Let the Children Come to Me

And people were bringing children to him that he might touch them, but the disciples rebuked them. When Jesus saw this he became indignant and said to them, "Let the children come to me; do not prevent them, for the kingdom of God belongs to such as these. Amen, I say to you, whoever does not accept the kingdom of God like a child will not enter it." Then he embraced them and blessed them, placing his hands on them.

Mark 10:13-16

Jesus sent a very important message that day that the kingdom of God belongs to everyone, even the smallest members of our parishes. Parents and their families continue to join the crowd of people who come to hear the Word of God proclaimed and celebrated. They come to receive God's blessing on their lives and on the lives of their children.

Our parishes are enriched by our children and grandchildren and by those of friends and visitors. Every one of these children is born with a sense of God's presence. The toddler stage is a fitting time to talk about God's love for the child and about Jesus, the caring friend God has sent. It is important for the parents and the Church to nurture this sense of God's presence. The seeds of faith will grow quickly in our little ones with the support of parents and the parish community. For the toddler, "church" often means the nursery, where God's love is experienced in the attention, smiles, and hugs of their caregivers. The parents entrust their precious little ones to people who will care for them in a welcoming and safe environment that will nurture their faith.

Welcoming Little Ones is your companion to providing a faith-filled nursery for toddlers ages twelve months to thirty-six months and their parents. In this resource you will find the practical ideas and information you need to coordinate a welcoming and safe nursery ministry. In addition, you will find twenty-three experiential sessions filled with age appropriate activities that will sow the seeds of faith and love in your toddlers, letting them grow under the loving touch of the Holy Spirit.

Building a Program

The nursery sessions

The individual sessions include stories, games, patterns, crafts, songs, ritual, and short age-appropriate prayers. There is also a variety of fun and imaginative activities, all designed for the toddler and caregiver. For each session you will find a caregiver insight page, comprehensive instructions for the various activities, and a reproducible family note that goes home each week with the toddlers.

The easy-to-use sessions are flexible and quickly adaptable to your nursery program as you choose specific activities tailored to fit the needs your toddlers and staff. Each session is approximately one hour long and can be easily led by one caregiver and helpers, or by a team of caregivers sharing the fun and responsibility. Session plans can be read quickly, and many of the ideas may be used immediately.

Appropriate toddler themes

As Christians we recognize that all of creation is a gift. Everything comes to us from the caring hand of God. The toddler is just beginning to discover some of the wonderful things God has given His people. The core nursery sessions follow the days of creation and explore some of the many gifts with which God has filled our world. In time the young child will begin to see God's love in the gifts of creation.

Welcoming the Little Ones

In addition to the fifteen core lessons there are plans for a welcome session and seven complete seasonal sessions including: Thanksgiving, Advent, Christmas, Valentine's Day, Lent, Easter, and summer.

The pages that follow will introduce you to what a toddler is like, offer a general list of caregiver responsibilities, and give step-by-step instructions on how to plan a successful session with the toddlers. Tools for teaching toddlers will give positive reinforcement as you share your faith and God's love with the children.

Extra essentials — ABC

❑ Section A offers strategies for organizing the nuts and bolts of your nursery. The topics include promotion ideas, opening and closing checklists, and many reproducible aids, such as a registration form and information sheet.

❑ In Section B, toddlers are the topic. You will find tips for everything from settling a crying toddler to serving snacks. The chapter is arranged for quick reference to help you with a variety of toddler needs.

❑ Section C provides resource listings, such as supplies to collect and easily implemented ideas for nursery games, songs, and movement.

Put all of these together and you will have a faith-filled nursery where parents have confidence that their toddler is being well-cared-for and that the seeds of faith are being nurtured in their little ones.

I Am A Toddler
Twelve to Thirty-six Months

I am . . .
A joy to be with
Full of energy and on the go
Always learning
Curious but with a short attention span
Quickly developing large-muscle skills
Working on fine-motor tasks
Becoming assertive in my environment
Lovingly and openly sharing all my emotions

I learn . . .
Using my senses
Through repetition
Imitating role models
By doing and discovering
Through exploration and imagination

I want . . .
A safe environment and physical care
Unconditional love and approval
A stimulating environment and experiences
Social opportunities
Security and predictability

Growing Seeds of Faith

The seeds of faith will grow as the toddler experiences love, attention, and guidance. This consistent, patient nurturing helps the young child grow into an awareness that he or she is loved. As the seeds continue to grow the child will recognize God as loving, forgiving, and accepting.

The toddler is just beginning to discover some of the wonderful things God created. In time the young child will see God's love in the gifts of creation. The toddler's sense of ritual in the nursery welcomes opportunities to sing, to play, to hear stories, and to share snack. These rituals are the beginning of belonging to a loving parish family that knows and cares about him or her. These seeds will grow into trusting that he or she is a beloved child of God.

Welcome to the Nursery Ministry Team!

Thank you for being an important part of this great ministry. You will be helping to lay the foundation of faith in the toddlers you care for. As you share God's loving care with the little ones you will be rewarded with giggles and hugs.

General Caregiver Responsibilities:

1. Ahead of time, familiarize yourself with the session activity plan you have been given.
2. Arrive fifteen minutes before the nursery is scheduled to open. Set up the room, checking on and organizing materials. Please wear the name tag provided to identify you as one of the caregivers.
3. Welcome parents and children as they arrive. Answer any questions and receive any special instructions the parents may have. Engage the children in the activities of the morning.
4. Be involved in the activities of the nursery and the care of the toddlers. Be attentive to any signs of hunger or discomfort.
5. As the parents arrive for pick-up of their child, take a minute to tell them about their toddler's morning.
6. Help with general clean-up.
7. Pray for the toddlers and their families.

Please remember:
❑ You may not give any medication to any child.
❑ Do not let a toddler leave with someone who is not listed on the toddler's information sheet.
❑ Toddlers may not be left alone at any time.
❑ If you are sick, please call the coordinator as soon as possible so that a substitute may be arranged.

Notes for Caregiver to Record and Keep...

Nursery Coordinator's Name: _____

Office phone number: _____ Home phone number: _____

Other Nursery Caregivers:

Name: _____ Phone number: _____

Name: _____ Phone number: _____

Substitutes:

Name_____ Phone number: _____

Name: _____ Phone number: _____

Dates I am scheduled to work in the nursery:

September_____ October _____

November _____ December _____

January _____ February _____

March _____ April _____

May _____ June _____

July _____ August _____

Important information

First aid is located: _____

Emergency phone numbers are located: _____

Custodial equipment is stored: _____

Disinfectant and cleaning solutions are stored: _____

Emergency exit plans are posted: _____

Emergency exits are located: _____

Trash and diapers are disposed of by: _____

Hand-washing sinks are found: _____

Toddler's names and home phone numbers

_____ _____

_____ _____

_____ _____

_____ _____

_____ _____

_____ _____

Tools for Teaching Toddlers

Have a positive attitude
- Be enthusiastic as you share your faith with toddlers.
- Be patient as you work with toddlers who are just learning how to communicate their thoughts and feelings.
- Be understanding of spilt juice, loud giggles, and tears.
- Be open to God's guidance in the nursery and see God's presence in each toddler.
- Offer loving guidance and direction to the toddlers.

Help your toddlers feel safe
- Be attentive to their basic needs for food and comfort.
- Provide ample room for the toddlers to move and play in groups or as individuals.
- Supply adequate and consistent supervision. Toddlers are assured and persistent explorers.

They are not yet aware of the consequences of their actions.

Express God's love
- ♥ Call each toddler by name.
- ♥ Kneel or sit down to be at eye-level to talk or play with the toddlers.
- ♥ Tell the toddlers that you are happy to see them and are glad they came to church.
- ♥ When conversing with a toddler keep your language simple and be a good listener. One can easily be distracted in the nursery.
- ♥ Pat their heads, hold their hands, and hug them often.
- ♥ Pray for each one of the toddlers and tell them you are doing so.

They may not understand exactly what you are doing, but they will know they have a special connection to you. Most importantly, tell the toddlers often that God loves each of them very much.

Planning the Session

Read over the caregiver's page for an overview of the session.

❑ The Scripture section will give you the Bible reference for the session.

❑ Use the background information to give you an understanding of the theme and the connections for toddlers of the lesson.

❑ Offer the prayer as a beginning to opening yourself to God's guidance as you plan the session.

❑ Check the session options for an assortment of learning activities from which to choose. The needed materials are specified directly below each listed activity.

❑ Read over the session carefully. Choose and circle the activities that will work best for you and the toddlers, or use a highlighter to mark the activities.

Keep in mind...
❑ The welcome offers an activity to engage the toddlers' interest and to introduce them to the theme of the session.

❑ The song, story, game, and art or craft suggestions make the theme experiential.

❑ The short prayer provides a reflection or prayer of thanksgiving for the toddlers to repeat phrase by phrase.

❑ The wrap-up will help you to review the theme at the end of the session until the parents arrive.

Gather the materials, assemble props, and make copies of the weekly family note, "Today In the Nursery."

This short note will provide parents with information about the day's theme, nursery activities, and related family activities. On the reverse side of the family note, there is a simple form to inform parents of the individual care of their child (page 11). During the session take a few moments to fill in the information for each toddler.

Welcoming the Little Ones

Remember as you plan...

Fun-loving toddlers will move quickly from one activity to another as they explore and create.

Being familiar with all the options in the session will offer you flexibility. If the plan isn't working, change the plan. Don't expect more than a few minutes of group time.

Anticipate several activities going on at a time in the nursery. Since toddlers may need a personal telling of a story or finger play, solicit help from your aides or helpers.

Assembling the Weekly Information and Family Notes

1. The last page of each session contains two copies of the weekly family note. Copy this page on a sheet of brightly colored 8-1/2" x 11" paper.

2. On the opposite page you'll find two copies of the weekly information sheet. Copy this page on the reverse side of the weekly family notes.

3. Cut the sheets in half so you get two notes from each sheet. The family note will be on one side and the information form on the other.

4. During the session, take a brief moment to fill in each child's name on the space provided.

5. Communicate each child's individual activity in the nursery by writing short comments for the three areas: "played," "snacked," and "diapered."

6. Place the completed weekly note with the child's belongings or distribute it to parents as the child departs.

What _____ did today!

Played:

Snacked:

Diapered:

What _____ did today!

Played:

Snacked:

Diapered:

Weekly Information Sheet/Family Note Assembly Instructions

1. The last page of each session contains two copies of the weekly family note. Copy this page on a sheet of brightly colored 8-1/2" x 11" paper.

2. On the opposite side of this page you'll find two copies of the weekly information sheet. Copy this page on the reverse side of the weekly family notes.

3. Cut the sheets in half so you get two notes from each sheet. The family note will be on one side and the information form on the other.

4. During the session take a brief moment to fill in each child's name on the space provided.

5. Communicate each child's individual activity in the nursery by writing short comments for the three areas: "played," "snacked," and "diapered."

6. Place the completed weekly note with the child's belongings or distribute it to parents as the child departs.

Jesus, Our Friend, Welcomes Us

"People were bringing even infants to him that he might touch them, and when the disciples saw this, they rebuked them. Jesus, however, called the children to himself and said, 'Let the children come to me and do not prevent them; for the kingdom of God belongs to such as these. Amen, I say to you, whoever does not accept the kingdom of God like a child will not enter it.' "

Luke 18:15-17

Dear Caregiver,

It was the custom for parents to bring their children to the rabbi to be blessed. That is exactly what the parents wanted for their children from Jesus. The disciples could see how tired Jesus was and didn't want him to be bothered. But Jesus gathered the little ones, putting his hand on each one and blessing them. Jesus welcomed the little children when others did not. The nursery is a place for the toddlers to experience God's love and to get acquainted with their friend, Jesus, while enjoying the companionship of other toddlers and adults. Getting accustomed to a new routine and new surroundings may take time for some toddlers. As you plan for this session be reminded that knowing Jesus as a friend will provide needed comfort to all those who visit the nursery.

Session Options and Materials
❏ Follow-the-Leader game
❏ picture of Jesus (preferably with children)
❏ "Do You Know Who Jesus Is?" song
❏ "Jesus Welcomes the Little Children" story
  ✗ flannel-board patterns on page 123
❏ Jesus medallions craft
  ✗ a juice-can lid for each child
  ✗ permanent marker for adult use
  ✗ at least one sticker of Jesus for each child
❏ "Keep Me Near You" prayer
❏ Torn-paper collage group activity
  ✗ variety of tissue and wrapping paper scraps
  ✗ paste
  ✗ red tag-board
  ✗ scissors
❏ Copied family note for each child

A Prayer for You
Jesus, my friend, grant me a joyful heart and patience as I help your cherished children become familiar with a new routine and new surroundings. Like you, let me be energized by these children, who come to the nursery for playful fun, loving care, and gentle comfort.
Amen.

Session One — Welcome to the Nursery!
Jesus, Our Friend, Welcomes Us
Sing the "Hello Song" found on page 119.

Welcome

Follow the Leader
Play follow the leader with the children while chanting the following rhyme:
> We're following the leader,
> The leader, the leader.
> We're following the leader
> Where-ever she/he may go.

Begin with the teacher leading the group in some silly actions (swaying like a monkey, flying like an airplane, patting head, rubbing tummy, etc.), then invite others to lead us as the children seem comfortable with the activity. Introduce the children to a picture of Jesus. Tell the children Jesus is God's Son. He loves them very much. Jesus wants them to feel happy when they come to visit the nursery. If possible keep a picture displayed each week of Jesus welcoming the children.

Song

Do You Know Who Jesus Is?
Sing to the tune of "Do You Know the Muffin Man?"

> Oh, do you know
> Who Jesus is?
> Who Jesus is?
> Who Jesus is?
> Oh, do you know
> Who Jesus is?
> Yes! Jesus is my friend!

For more verses replace "Jesus" with the names of toddlers.

Prayer

Keep Me Near You
Show the children how you fold your hands as you say this prayer.

> Jesus, you are my friend.
> Keep me near you always.
> Amen.

Story

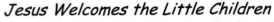

Jesus Welcomes the Little Children
Jesus talked about God's great love to many people. After a while, he got very tired and needed to rest. The moms and dads were tired and hungry too, but they wanted their children to see Jesus. Some of the other people told the moms and dads, "Go away! Jesus is too tired." Jesus heard this and said, "Let the little children come to me." So the little children came to Jesus and he reached out to them and said, "I want to be your friend."

Tell this delightful flannel-board story to the toddlers. Use the flannel-board patterns on page 123.

Craft
Jesus medallions

Using a permanent marker, write "Jesus is my friend" on one side of a juice-can lid. Provide a variety of stickers with pictures of Jesus for the children to select from. Invite the toddlers to put their choice of sticker on the back of the lid. Give the children their medallions to keep in their pockets as a reminder that Jesus wants to be their friend.

Jesus medallion

Wrap-up

Torn-paper collage

Cut a large heart from red poster-board. Write the message "Jesus is our friend" across the heart. Say each child's name as you print it on the heart. Have ready a basketful of colorful tissue and gift-wrap paper for the toddlers to tear and paste anywhere on the heart. As you complete this activity, say to the group, "Jesus is a friend to all of us and is happy you have come to the nursery today."

Torn-paper collage

Sing the "Good-bye Song" or "Blessing Song" found on page 119.

Welcome to the Nursery!
Jesus, Our Friend, Welcomes Us

Today's Nursery Song

Sing to the tune of "Do You Know the Muffin Man?"

Oh, do you know
Who Jesus is?
Who Jesus is?
Who Jesus is?
Oh, do you know
Who Jesus is?
Yes! Jesus is my friend!

Today in the Nursery

We talked about our friend, Jesus. We played follow the leader and made medallions.

Family Activity

Share pictures and storybooks about Jesus with your toddler. Discuss how as Christians we are followers of him — how we try to be like him.

Welcome to the Nursery!
Jesus, Our Friend, Welcomes Us

Today's Nursery Song

Sing to the tune of "Do You Know the Muffin Man?"

Oh, do you know
Who Jesus is?
Who Jesus is?
Who Jesus is?
Oh, do you know
Who Jesus is?
Yes! Jesus is my friend!

Today in the Nursery

We talked about our friend, Jesus. We played follow the leader and made medallions.

Family Activity

Share pictures and storybooks about Jesus with your toddler. Discuss how as Christians we are followers of him — how we try to be like him.

Earth Was Covered in Darkness

"In the beginning, when God created the heavens and the earth, the earth was a formless wasteland, and darkness covered the abyss, while a mighty wind swept over the waters."
Genesis 1:1-2

Dear Caregiver,

In the beginning the world was a dark place. There were no people or plants or animals. There were no sun, no moon, or stars. There wasn't even any sky or earth. Only God. Toddlers see darkness when covering their eyes to play "peek-a-boo," when hiding objects under a blanket, or at night when the lights are turned down for a restful sleep. This session, the toddlers will further explore the darkness of tunnels and caves. Moving toy cars and stuffed animals through cardboard-carton caves and paper-tube tunnels will be an exciting adventure for the toddlers. With the help of their vivid imaginations, the toddlers will further investigate darkness. Moving away from the darkness, they will learn and see more of what God has created.

Session Options and Materials
❏ Tubes, cartons, and cylinders discovery activity
❏ a crate or box filled with various-sized paper-towel tubes and cardboard cartons
❏ toy cars and small, stuffed animals
❏ "In the Dark I Cannot See" song
❏ "A Bear Inside the Cave" story
❏ Tunnels, cars, and caves exploration activity
  ✗ scissors for leader's use
  ✗ masking tape to create roads and paths
  ✗ a parachute or a fitted bedsheet
❏ "Dark of Night" prayer
❏ Parachute movement
❏ Copied family note for each child

A Prayer for You
God, from the darkness you have created a world full of life, wonder, and love. Help me to open the children's eyes to the world you have created, their minds to your wonder, and their hearts to your love. Amen.

Day One of Creation
Earth Was Covered in Darkness

Sing the "Hello Song" found on page 119.

Welcome

Tubes, cartons, and cylinders

When the children arrive, set out a crate of cars, stuffed or plastic toy animals, tubes, cartons, and cylinders for the toddlers to play with. After they have had a chance explore these materials, hide the toy cars and animals under and inside the containers. Make it a game of seek and find. Ask the children, "Where is the ____?" Give clues and ask questions which will lead them to the object.

Song

In the Dark I Cannot See
Sing to the tune of "London Bridge"

In the dark I cannot see,
Cannot see,
Cannot see.
Leave the dark and I will see
All God's given me.

Invite the children to cover their eyes for the first two lines of the song. When they uncover their eyes for the last two lines, the leader points to a person or object in the room and whispers to the children, "Who's (or what's) this?" The leader may sing their reply, "God's given us Terry."

Prayer

Dark of Night
Invite the toddlers to use their hands to cover their eyes as they repeat the prayer, one line at a time.

Thank you for the dark that hides the sun so we may rest at night. Amen.

Story

Bear Inside the Cave

Use a soft, stuffed animal and an empty carton to retell this story. Fold the opening flaps of the carton inside to form a cave.

When it gets dark outside and the animals are tired from their day of play, they look for a spot to sleep. A soft, cuddly bear can hardly keep his tired eyes open. He needs a place to rest. He looks inside a hollow tree but it is too small for him to fit inside. Moving along the path, the tired bear comes to the opening of a big, dark cave. Not able to see, he uses his paws to feel around inside the dark cave. He bumps into the sides of the cave until he finds a cozy spot to curl up into a ball. There the little bear rests until morning.

Craft
Tunnels, cars, and caves

Connect the tunnels (tubes and cylinders) and caves (cartons) together by roads and paths made of masking tape. Help the toddlers to play with toy cars, people, and animals, moving them in and out of the dark tunnels and caves. Talk about the darkness inside the tunnels and caves. Give toddlers cylinders that have been cut in half (as shown below) to decorate with dark crayons. Send their decorated cylinder home for them to use with their families.

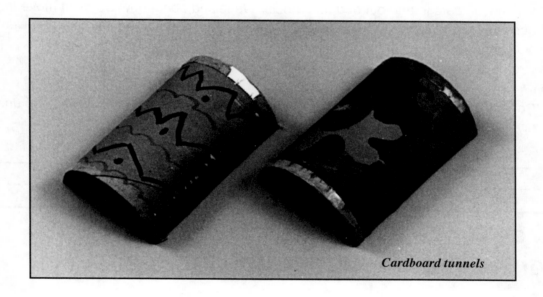

Cardboard tunnels

Wrap-up

Parachute fun
Practice following directions

Spread out a parachute (or fitted bedsheet) in an open area of the room. Invite the toddlers to bring objects to place on or under the parachute. Give other directions as to where they might place the objects. Then as a group, holding the edges of the parachute, lift it up over your heads and crawl under it. Some children will need a few times of watching others participate before they actually take part in the fun.

Sing the "Good-bye Song" or "Blessing Song" found on page 119.

Day One of Creation
Earth Was Covered in Darkness

Today's Nursery Song
Sing to the tune of "London Bridge"
In the dark I cannot see,
Cannot see, cannot see.
Leave the dark and I will see
All God's given me.

Today in the Nursery
We moved cars in and out of dark tunnels. We talked about how we must move from darkness to see the world God has made. We also heard a story about a bear that went into a dark cave to rest.

Family Activity
Cover your eyes with your hands and play peekaboo with your child. When you uncover your eyes, talk about all you see that God has given you.

Day One of Creation
Earth Was Covered in Darkness

Today's Nursery Song
Sing to the tune of "London Bridge"
In the dark I cannot see,
Cannot see, cannot see.
Leave the dark and I will see
All God's given me.

Today in the Nursery
We moved cars in and out of dark tunnels. We talked about how we must move from darkness to see the world God has made. We also heard a story about a bear that went into a dark cave to rest.

Family Activity
Cover your eyes with your hands and play peekaboo with your child. When you uncover your eyes, talk about all you see that God has given you.

Session Three — Day One of Creation
God Gives Us Light

"Then God said 'Let there be light,' and there was light. God saw how good the light was. God then separated the light from the darkness. God called the light 'day,' and the darkness he called 'night.' Thus evening came, and morning followed — the first day."

Genesis 1:3-5

Session Options and Materials
- ❑ Flashlights light the darkness activity
  - ✖ paper-tube tunnels and cardboard-carton caves from Session Two
  - ✖ masking tape
  - ✖ toy cars and stuffed animals
  - ✖ flashlight
- ❑ "Shine the Light So I Can See" song
- ❑ "Morning Light Wakes the Bear" story
- ❑ Picture viewer craft
  - ✖ 5½-by-8½-inch stiff paper for each child to make viewer (see pattern, page 23)
- ❑ "Waking with Light" prayer
- ❑ "What's this…?" activity
  - ✖ picture books
- ❑ Copied family note for each child

Dear Caregiver,

God had a wonderful plan — a plan to make the world and all that is in it. God made all of creation, and God's creation continues to flourish. God gives us light to separate the day from night. For toddlers, the morning light is usually what awakens them at the start of a new day. Light is turned on in their rooms so they may find a special toy or look at a favorite book. Session Three of Day One uses a flashlight to illuminate the darkness of the tunnels and caves used in Session Two. The toddlers' exploration of light and dark continues as the flashlight is shined on people and objects around the room with which God has blessed us.

A Prayer for You
God, you said, "Let there be light." As I explore the topics of darkness and light with little ones, let my words and actions light the way for others to find your love. Amen.

Day One of Creation
God Gives Us Light
Sing the "Hello Song" found on page 119.

Welcome
Flashlights light the darkness
As the children arrive, provide the tunnels and caves (boxes, cartons, and cylinders from Session One) to play with. Use masking tape to recreate the roads and paths for the cars and animals to travel. If the room allows, turn off the lights and illuminate the room with natural window lighting. Then introduce flashlights to the play by showing the toddlers how the flashlight beam lights up the darkness inside the tunnels and caves.

Song
Shine the Light So I Can See
Sing to the tune of "London Bridge"

Shine the light so I can see,
I can see, I can see.
Shine the light so I can see
All God's given me.

As you and the children sing the first three lines of the song, move the shining light around the room like a spotlight. On the last line of the song, stop the light beam on an object or person. Say with the children "God has given us (name the person or object)."

Prayer
Waking With Light
When you teach this prayer to the toddlers you may also teach them the sign for "day" as shown below.

Thank you, God, for waking us with daylight. Amen.

Story
Morning Light Wakes the Bear
Use the same stuffed animal and carton cave from Session One to retell this story.
The light from outside shines into the cave where the cuddly bear is sleeping. The bright light tells the sleepy bear it is morning time. Time to eat and play! The bear wakes up and rubs his eyes. He peeks out of the dark cave to see the world. What can the cuddly bear see outside the cave?

Craft
Picture viewer

Copy the pattern below on stiff 5½-by-8½-inch paper for each child. Cut away the viewing circle. Give each toddler the paper and a bright crayon to add a shining light. Use the picture viewer to look in books and magazines for objects the child can name. The open circle will help the toddler focus on a single object. As you look at the objects through the viewer, ask the child "What is this?" Then after some practice try introducing the phrase "God has given us _____." Send this home for the families to use, too.

Wrap-up

What's this...?

Use the flashlight to point to objects and people in the room. Ask the toddlers who or what the objects are.

Using their answer to fill in the blank, the leader may respond "God gives us light and we can see...." The more practice at this activity, the easier it will be for the toddlers to mimic.

Sing the "Good-bye Song" or "Blessing Song" found on page 119.

- -

See what God has given me.

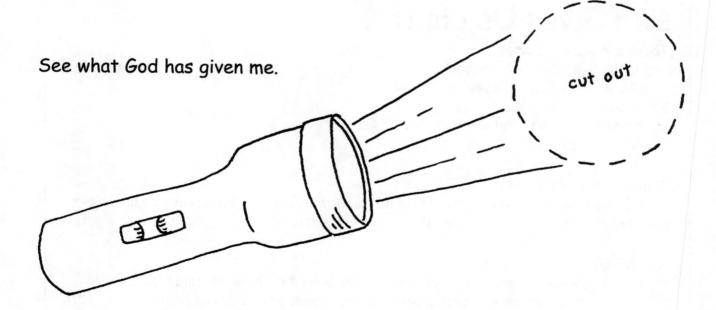

cut out

Day One of Creation
God Gives Us Light

Today's Nursery Song
Sing to the tune of "London Bridge"
Shine the light so I can see,
I can see, I can see.
Shine the light so I can see
All God's given me.

Today in the Nursery
We used flashlights to light up all God has made for us to see. We talked about how the light of morning wakes us up for the day.

Family Activity
Play a game of "What's this?" with your toddler using the viewer we made today. Slide the viewer across magazine or book pictures to find objects your child can name.

- -

Day One of Creation
God Gives Us Light

Today's Nursery Song
Sing to the tune of "London Bridge"
Shine the light so I can see,
I can see, I can see.
Shine the light so I can see
All God's given me.

Today in the Nursery
We used flashlights to light up all God has made for us to see. We talked about how the light of morning wakes us up for the day.

Family Activity
Play a game of "What's this?" with your toddler using the viewer we made today. Slide the viewer across magazine or book pictures to find objects your child can name.

From the Waters God Gives Us...

"Then God said, 'Let there be a dome in the middle of the waters, to separate one body of water from the other.'"
Genesis 1:6

Dear Caregiver,

Water is what gives life to the earth. Refreshing water to drink, cleansing water to bathe, life-giving water to grow, and renewing water to fill the seas and lakes. In our Baptism to the Catholic Church, these same characteristics serve as images for the life-giving waters of Baptism. To toddlers, water can be an everyday occurrence — water in a cup, water on a cloth, water for the plants, water in a tub. While providing some "splish-splashing" fun, build on the toddlers' experience with water and continue to focus on its life-giving qualities.

Session Options and Materials
- ❑ Washing and splashing play
  - ✖ basins, buckets, or tubs to hold water
  - ✖ small towels and wash cloths or sponges
  - ✖ toys to be washed
- ❑ "When I Get Thirsty" action song
- ❑ "Splashes of Water" story
  - ✖ pitchers and/or watering cans
  - ✖ small paper cups
  - ✖ paper towels
- ❑ Squirt water-bottle and chalk art activity
  - ✖ chalk
  - ✖ water squirt-bottle
  - ✖ construction paper
- ❑ "God Gives Us Splashing" water prayer
- ❑ Watering plants and animals activity
- ❑ Copied family note for each child

A Prayer for You
God, you fill my life with good things. Like a thirst-quenching glass of cool water, I am refreshed with the thoughts, words, and actions of the young children as their minds are opened to your greatness. Amen.

Welcoming the Little Ones

Day Two of Creation
From the Waters God Gives Us...
Sing the "Hello Song" found on page 119.

Welcome

Washing and splashing

Before the children arrive collect a group of toys that are washable. As the children arrive, invite them to help you place a small amount of water in wash tubs, basins, or ice-cream buckets. Set the containers of water on towels spread over the floor. Provide small wash cloths for washing and towels for drying. As you and the children wash the toys, talk about how water is used to wash away the dirt. Let the toddlers continue to explore the water. Provide them with containers to fill and from which to pour water.

Song
When I Get So Thirsty
Sing to the tune of "I'm a Little Teapot"

God puts the clean water in my cup.
(*pouring motion into fist*)
When I get so thirsty
I drink it up.
(*tip hand in a cup shape to mouth*)
Down my throat, to tummy it will go.
(*point to throat down neck, to tummy*)
Thank you God, water makes me grow.
(*stretch up straight and tall*)

Prayer
Splashing Water
Gently splash water in a bowl as you say this prayer.

God, we can do so much with the water you have given us. We splash, we drink, we wash, and we grow. Amen!

Story

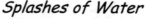

Splashes of Water
Use an empty basin to tell this story.

The rain from the sky fills the lake with clear fresh water. (*Pour some water from a pitcher into the empty basin.*) Thirsty people and animals come to drink the fresh water. (*Pour tiny drinks of water into cups for the children from the pitcher.*) When people need to wash away the dirt they see the water to wash their face. (*Wet paper towels for each child to wipe their own face.*) And on a hot day everyone loves to splash and play in the cool water. (*Invite the children to splash their hands in the basin of water.*)

Craft
Squirting water and chalk art

Using water in a spray bottle, help the toddlers to mist a sheet of construction paper. Give the toddlers chalk to scribble on the wet paper and create their own design. For older toddlers you may pre-copy a design on the paper before they squirt it with the water. Then provide chalk for these toddlers to trace over the preprinted design. After the activity help the toddlers to wipe the tables clean with sponges and water.

Chalk art

Wrap-up
Watering plants and animals

Fill a watering can or pitcher with water. With the help of the toddlers, water any plants in the room or building that need water. Refresh any animal's supply of water, too. Talk about how God has given us water to drink and how we need water to grow. As the water is poured for the plants or animals, you may teach the children this water rhyme, "I want you to know, it is God's water that helps us to grow. Thank you, God!"

Sing the "Good-bye Song" or "Blessing Song" found on page 119.

Day Two of Creation
From the Waters God Gives Us...

Today's Action Song
When I Get So Thirsty
Sing to the tune of "I'm a Little Teapot"
God puts the clean water in my cup.
(*pouring motion into fist*)
When I get so thirsty I drink it up.
(*tip hand in a cup shape to mouth*)
Down my throat and to tummy it will go.
Thank you God, water makes me grow.
(*stretch up straight and tall*)

Today in the Nursery
We splashed and washed toys in water. As we were refreshed with a cool drink of water we heard a story about some of the many ways water is used. Then we thanked God for all that we can do with water.

Family Activity
♥ Invite your toddler to help as you water house plants and replenish water for family pets.
♥ As your toddler splashes in his/her bath, sprinkle water on his/her head and say "May our life be sprinkled with God's love."

Day Two of Creation
From the Waters God Gives Us...

Today's Action Song
When I Get So Thirsty
Sing to the tune of "I'm a Little Teapot"
God puts the clean water in my cup.
(*pouring motion into fist*)
When I get so thirsty I drink it up.
(*tip hand in a cup shape to mouth*)
Down my throat and to tummy it will go.
Thank you God, water makes me grow.
(*stretch up straight and tall*)

Today in the Nursery
We splashed and washed toys in water. As we were refreshed with a cool drink of water we heard a story about some of the many ways water is used. Then we thanked God for all that we can do with water.

Family Activity
♥ Invite your toddler to help as you water house plants and replenish water for family pets.
♥ As your toddler splashes in his/her bath, sprinkle water on his/her head and say "May our life be sprinkled with God's love."

Session Five — Day Two of Creation
God Gives Us the Sky

"And so it happened: God made the dome from the water below it. God called the dome 'the sky.' Evening came, and morning followed — the second day."

Genesis 1:7-8

Dear Caregiver,

Even on a cloud-covered day, looking up to the vast sky we can see God's power has no limits. It is like a beautiful blanket of air and clouds that we often refer to as heaven. Looking at the sky from a toddler's view is seeing something very big and very far away. Bring God's sky closer for the toddlers with activities that will nurture their minds, bodies, and spirits, while enjoying the companionship of other toddlers. This session mixes exercise, dance, art, and parachute play together under the theme of "sky."

Session Options and Materials
- ❑ Sky collage
  - ✗ large sheets of white and blue construction paper
  - ✗ adult scissors
  - ✗ cotton balls
  - ✗ paste
  - ✗ foil
- ❑ Sky circle dance
- ❑ Stretching-for-the-sky exercise
- ❑ Shaving-cream art
  - ✗ shaving cream
  - ✗ paint shirts or plastic aprons for toddlers
- ❑ "Look Down On Us" prayer
- ❑ Parachute sky-play
  - ✗ parachute or twin-fitted sheet
- ❑ Copied family note for each child

A Prayer for You
I want to bring the children closer to you, God. I want them to learn all about your majesty and power. The heavenly sky is but one reminder your presence in our lives. Continue to be with us as we explore your creation. Amen.

Day Two of Creation
God Gives Us the Sky

Sing the "Hello Song" found on page 119.

Welcome

Sky-collage group art

As the toddlers arrive, invite them to assist in creating a sky collage as a group. At first just let the toddlers explore soft cotton-balls, encouraging them to pull and stretch them. As they explore, cut a large sheet of white construction paper into a cloud shape and place it on a low table for the toddlers to work at. Begin pasting the pulled

Sky collage

and stretched cotton balls on the cutout. Use this time to ask, "Where we can find white, fluffy clouds?" Go to a window and look in the sky to see if some clouds can be found. Next, paste the cloud to a large sheet of blue construction paper. Say to the toddlers, "God made the sky to hold the clouds." Cut a few droplet shapes from foil and ask the toddlers what these look like and where they fall from. Let toddlers help paste the foil droplets on the sky collage too.

Song
Sky circle-dance
Sing to the tune of "Skip to My Lou," holding hands and moving in a circle.

> Clouds up in the sky so blue,
> Holding water for me and you.
> (*mist group with water sprayer*)
> Rain falls down,
> (*group all falls down*)
> What'll we do? (*look at each other*)
> Dance with joy,
> (*group jumps up to dance*)
> Give thanks to God.

Prayer
Look Down On Us
Invite the children to repeat each line and do the actions.

> God in heaven,
> (*reach up*)
> Look down and smile at us
> (*bring arms down*)
> As we stretch and jump
> (*stretch and jump*)
> Under the big blue sky.

Rhyme

Stretching for the sky, invite the toddlers to do the movements with you as you say this rhyme.

I can stretch for the big blue sky.
Stretching, stretching, way up high.
I can jump to the clouds so white,
Jumping, jumping out of sight.
I can splash in the wet raindrops,

Splashing, splashing, then it stops.
Now I look to God's great heaven,
Thanking God for all that's given.
Sky — clouds — rain!
Thank you, God.

Craft
Shaving-cream art

Provide paint shirts or plastic aprons for each child participating in this activity.

On a low table squirt a small amount of shaving cream for each child to play with. As the children explore this medium, talk about what the clouds look like and how the toddlers think they might feel. Encourage the children to:

- use their fingers to draw,
- use their hands to smear,
- mimic lines made by the caregiver,
- scoop up a pile to create a new cloud.

Shaving cream art

Wrap-up

Parachute sky

As a closing activity, use a parachute to create a dome for the children to crawl under. Gather around the edge of a parachute or fitted sheet. With at least two adults grasping the edges, the group moves in a circle around the parachute. The toddlers can put cotton balls in the center and these can be bounced up and down by gently shaking the edges of the parachute. On the count of three — one-two-three! — the adults then lift the sheet high over their heads and release the parachute, creating a dome for the children to crawl under. Encourage the toddlers to try to crawl under the sheet before it falls to the floor. When everyone who wishes to be under the sheet is there, say "God saw the sky and said it was good."

Sing the "Good-bye Song" or "Blessing Song" found on page 119.

Day Two of Creation
God Gives Us the Sky

Today's Circle Game — Sky Dance
Sing to the tune of "Skip to My Lou"

Clouds up in the sky so blue,
Holding water for me and you.
Rain falls down,
What'll we do?
Dance with joy,
Give thanks to God.

O Lord, my God you are great indeed.
Psalm 104:1

Today in the Nursery
We played, we danced, and we exercised to praise God, creator of the majestic skies.

Family Activity
With your toddler take a few moments to view the greatness of God's creation, the sky. Throw a blanket down on the ground and lie back to view the heavens. Talk about the shapes of the clouds and watch as they change before your eyes.

Day Two of Creation
God Gives Us the Sky

Today's Circle Game — Sky Dance
Sing to the tune of "Skip to My Lou"

Clouds up in the sky so blue,
Holding water for me and you.
Rain falls down,
What'll we do?
Dance with joy,
Give thanks to God.

O Lord, my God you are great indeed.
Psalm 104:1

Today in the Nursery
We played, we danced, and we exercised to praise God, creator of the majestic skies.

Family Activity
With your toddler take a few moments to view the greatness of God's creation, the sky. Throw a blanket down on the ground and lie back to view the heavens. Talk about the shapes of the clouds and watch as they change before your eyes.

Session Six — Day Three of Creation
God Gives Us Land and Sea

"Then God said, 'Let the water under the sky be gathered in a single basin, so that the dry land may appear.' And so it happened; the water under the sky was gathered into its basin, and the dry land appeared. God called the dry land 'the earth,' and the basin of water he called 'the sea.' God saw how good it was."

Genesis 1:9-10

Dear Caregiver,

God provides land and water to support all life on earth. Plants, animals, and people need dry land and wet waters to flourish. Toddlers enjoy the opportunity to poke, stir, push, and shape in mud or sand. While encouraging the development of toddlers' fine motor skills, digging in a basin of moist sand will stimulate conversation of another one of God's creations.

Session Options and Materials
- ❑ Sand-play activity
  - ✗ vinyl table cloth
  - ✗ basins or 9x13-inch baking pans
  - ✗ sand and sand toys
- ❑ "God Made the Mountaintops" song
- ❑ "God's Great Land" story
- ❑ Colored sand-art activity
  - ✗ colored chalk-scrapings
  - ✗ table salt
  - ✗ construction paper
  - ✗ paste
  - ✗ jelly-roll pan
- ❑ "Hills and Valleys" prayer
- ❑ Mountains and valleys play activity
  - ✗ sleeping bags
  - ✗ copied family note for each child

A Prayer for You
God, you have shaped and formed the land from rock, soil, and sand. Continue to shape my faith as I nurture the growing faith of the toddlers with your gentle love. Amen.

Day Three of Creation
God Gives Us Land and Sea
Sing the "Hello Song" found on page 119.

Welcome

Sand play
Place a vinyl tablecloth on the floor and provide basins or brownie-pans full of sand for the toddlers to explore. Prevent excessive dust by moistening the sand with water before playing in it. To encourage the exploration, give the toddlers scoops and shovels to dig with, containers to fill and pour from, and combs to make designs with. As the children poke, pat, mold, and shape the sand, talk how God made the valleys, mountains, and hills for us to climb and see over.

Song
God Made Mountaintops
Sing to the tune of "London Bridge" while pairs of children join hands to make an arch high or low according to the verse.

High up on the mountaintops
Mountain tops, mountaintops.
High up on the mountaintops we see _____.
(*Search around the room with hand shading over brow, have the toddlers fill in the blank with a word for something they see.*)
In the valleys God has made, God has made, God
   has made,
In the valleys God has made,
We can _____.
(*Invite the toddlers to suggest some movement like climb, jump, stomp, etc.*)

Prayer
Hills and Valleys
Encourage the toddlers to fold their hands, be quiet and still as you say this prayer.

God, you give us mountains to climb and valleys to play in. Thank you for the land. Amen.

Story

God's Great Land
Over the hills and faraway,
(*make bumpy hills with hand in a wavy motion, then shade eyes with hand over brow, searching*)
God made rivers here to stay.
(*form a river with hand in a wiggly motion*)
Down the river water flows
(*move hand in a sliding motion*)

Near by where the sea breeze blows.
(*give a gentle blow*)
God made land and rivers and seas,
Look to find the beauty in these.
(*shade eyes with hand over brow and pretend to search*)
Climb up over the rocks and sand
(*lift legs as though to climb*)
You will see the work of God's hands.
(*from chest reach hands out over the land*)

Craft
Colored sand

As preparation, scrape a variety of colored chalk. Mix the individual colors of chalk scrapings with table salt.

Give the toddler a sheet of construction paper in a jelly-roll pan. Using fingers and paste, invite them to create a design on the paper. Let the toddler select a color of chalk/salt mixture to sprinkle on the paste design. Lift paper and shake away any loose chalk/salt mixture over the jelly roll pan.

Colored sand

Wrap-up

Mountains and valleys

Fluff and shape a sleeping bag or two into a big fluffy pile. Encourage the toddlers to crawl up to the "top of the mountain." Then lay the sleeping bag flat and encourage the children to sit "down in the valley." Continue to make "mountains" and "valleys," each time thanking God for the mountains and valleys all over the land.

Sing the "Good-bye Song" or "Blessing Song" found on page 119.

Day Three of Creation

God Gives Us Land and Sea

Today's Action Song
God Made Mountaintops

Sing to the tune of "London Bridge" while pairs of children join hands to make an arch high or low according to the verse.

High up on the mountaintops
Mountain tops, mountaintops.
High up on the mountaintops we see _____.
In the valleys God has made, God has made, God has made,
In the valleys God has made,
We can _____ .

Today in the Nursery
We celebrated God's creation of land and sea as we dug sand and made mountains from sleeping bags.

Family Activity
Take a walk with your toddler to look for rocks, sand, and soil. Dig and make hills of sand or piles of the rocks. While playing, thank God for all the dry land we have on earth.

Day Three of Creation

God Gives Us Land and Sea

Today's Action Song
God Made Mountaintops

Sing to the tune of "London Bridge" while pairs of children join hands to make an arch high or low according to the verse.

High up on the mountaintops
Mountain tops, mountaintops.
High up on the mountaintops we see _____.
In the valleys God has made, God has made, God has made,
In the valleys God has made,
We can _____ .

Today in the Nursery
We celebrated God's creation of land and sea as we dug sand and made mountains from sleeping bags.

Family Activity
Take a walk with your toddler to look for rocks, sand, and soil. Dig and make hills of sand or piles of the rocks. While playing, thank God for all the dry land we have on earth.

God Gives Us Flowers and Grass

"Then God said, 'Let the earth bring forth vegetation: every kind of plant that bears seed and every kind of fruit tree on earth that bears fruit with its seed in it.'"
Genesis 1:11

Session Options and Materials
- ❑ Flower match game
- ❑ piece of tag-board
  - ✗ blue, red, yellow pieces of colored paper (cut into flower shapes)
- ❑ "Plant the Seed" action song
- ❑ "Tom and Tess" story
- ❑ Tom and Tess patterns (cut out of colored paper)
- ❑ Finger-paint garden art
  - ✗ finger paint
  - ✗ one or two large, plastic trays
  - ✗ dishpan with soapy water
  - ✗ paper towels
  - ✗ aprons
- ❑ "A Wonderful World" prayer
- ❑ Parachute flower activity
  - ✗ parachute or fitted bed-sheet
- ❑ Copied family note for each child

Dear Caregiver,

Toddlers are so excited about everyday adventures and discoveries of life. Watch their eyes light up and sparkle as they walk barefoot through the grass or smell a fragrant flower for the first time. It reminds us that all of God's beautiful creation is a reflection of God's generous love.

In this session the toddlers will find out that God caused the grass and the budding plants to grow. Through a game they will explore the variety of colors God used in making flowers. As they sing an action song the toddlers will be investigating the planting of seeds.

A Prayer for You

Generous God, let my heart and spirit be filled with your love as I see and experience creation through the eyes of the children. May I be a reflection of this boundless love to toddlers. Amen.

Day Three of Creation
God Gives Us Flowers and Grass
Sing the "Hello Song" found on page 119.

Welcome
Flower match game
Cut out four blue, four red, and four yellow paper-flowers. Glue two of each color on a large piece of poster-board. Put the others into a box. Sit down on the floor, inviting the children to join you. Ask the children, "Do you know what the objects on the poster-board are?" Tell the children there are many different kinds of flowers. Invite the children to take a flower out of the box and place it on the same colored flower on the board. When you have finished, tell the children that God made all the flowers, plants, and even the grass for us to enjoy.

Song
Plant the Seed
Sing to the tune of the "Here We Go 'Round the Mulberry Bush."

This is the way we plant the seed,
Plant the seed, plant the seed.
(*place the seed in hand*)
This is the way we plant the seed,
Digging a small hole.
(*dig a hole*)
Then we put the seed inside,
Seed inside, seed inside.
(*put seed in your hand*)
Then we put the seed inside
and cover it with dirt.
(*pretend to sprinkle over hand*)
The sun and rain will help it grow,
Help it grow, help it grow.
(*use hand to show it growing*)
The sun and rain will help it
grow into a beautiful flower.

Prayer
A Wonderful World
Have the children raise their hands in praise as they repeat the lines of this prayer.

Dear God, the flowers smell great, the grass is so soft, what a wonderful world you made! Amen.

Story
Tom and Tess

Tom and Tess went out to play. Tom said, "Let's play on the grass." Running, jumping, hopping, rolling are the things I like to do on the soft green grass. What do you like to do on the grass? (*Invite children to suggest other ideas.*)

Tess said "Well, I like the flowers." Looking, sniffing, counting all the colors are the things I like to do when the flowers are in bloom. What do you like to do when the flowers are in bloom?

Tom and Tess had a great day running and rolling on the grass, counting and sniffing all the flowers, too.

Craft
Finger-paint garden

Set some large plastic trays on a low table. Put waterproof aprons on the children who want to finger paint. Place a dishpan partially filled with soapy water and paper towels nearby to wash hands. Put one or two tablespoons of bright-colored finger-paint on each tray. Help each child get started by demonstrating how to move the paint around the paper. When the child seems finished, have him/her make hand-prints on a new paper. Then have the child wash their hands in the pan of soapy water. After the picture has dried a few minutes, with a marker add stems and leaves to the flower hands.

Wrap-up

Parachute flower

Gather the children around a fitted sheet or parachute. Place the paper flowers in the middle. Tell the children to pretend that the paper flowers are seeds they planted in the ground. Then the rain came and the seeds began to grow. With everyone holding the edges of the sheet, gently move the sheet in an upward and downward motion. Tell the children that sunshine followed the rain and the flowers grew and spread. Move the sheet in the same manner as before, but with a faster motion until the flowers have all blown off. Gather up the paper flowers and start all over again.

Sing the "Good-bye Song" or "Blessing Song" found on page 119.

Day Three of Creation
God Gives Us Flowers and Grass

Today's Action Song
Plant the Seed
Sing to the tune of the "Here We Go 'Round the Mulberry Bush."

This is the way we plant the seed,
Plant the seed, plant the seed.
This is the way we plant the seed,
Digging a small hole.
Then we put the seed inside,
Seed inside, seed inside.
Then we put the seed inside
and cover it with dirt.
The sun and rain will help it grow,
Help it grow, help it grow.
The sun and rain will help it
grow into a beautiful flower.

Today in the Nursery
We played a flower match game and talked about the many different colors and kinds of flowers God gives us. We made finger-paint gardens and sang a song about planting seeds.

Family Activity
Plant some seeds together outside or in a pot indoors. Encourage your toddler to water them carefully and watch them grow. Gently hold your child's hand in yours and say, "Dear God, the flowers smell great and the grass is so soft. What a wonderful world you made!"

Day Three of Creation
God Gives Us Flowers and Grass

Today's Action Song
Plant the Seed
Sing to the tune of the "Here We Go 'Round the Mulberry Bush."

This is the way we plant the seed,
Plant the seed, plant the seed.
This is the way we plant the seed,
Digging a small hole.
Then we put the seed inside,
Seed inside, seed inside.
Then we put the seed inside
and cover it with dirt.
The sun and rain will help it grow,
Help it grow, help it grow.
The sun and rain will help it
grow into a beautiful flower.

Today in the Nursery
We played a flower match game and talked about the many different colors and kinds of flowers God gives us. We made finger-paint gardens and sang a song about planting seeds.

Family Activity
Plant some seeds together outside or in a pot indoors. Encourage your toddler to water them carefully and watch them grow. Gently hold your child's hand in yours and say, "Dear God, the flowers smell great and the grass is so soft. What a wonderful world you made!"

God Gives Us Trees

"And so it happened: the earth brought forth every kind of plant that bears fruit with its seed on it. God saw how good it was."
Genesis 1:11-12

Session Options and Materials
❑ Tree-puzzle activity
  ✗ a flat sheet
  ✗ a bag with pieces of a tree (such as small branches, leaves, needles, bark)
  ✗ a large sheet of paper with a simple outline of a tree (see example)
❑ "Ring Around God's Tree" game
❑ Five trees finger-play
❑ Tree scribble-art
  ✗ masking tape
  ✗ a few scraps of sandpaper
  ✗ one sheet of paper per toddler
  ✗ green nontoxic markers or crayons
❑ "Trees Are Fun" prayer
❑ "Can you see?" activity
❑ Copied family note for each child

Dear Caregiver,
The desire for God in our lives is with us from our very beginnings. God continues to draw us near and make himself known to us. Beautiful leaves, branches dancing in the breeze, and bountiful fruit trees are all signs of God's loving and powerful presence. The toddlers will see God's presence as they put together a welcome puzzle and play "Can you see?"

A Prayer for You
Lord, you draw me near with your loving presence. I believe in you with the faith and will you have given me. Continue to open my eyes to your powerful presence and use me to spread your love to the children.

Day Three of Creation
God Gives Us Trees
Sing the "Hello Song" found on page 119.

Welcome

Tree puzzle

Put a flat sheet on the floor and invite the toddlers to come and sit around the sheet. In a bag have small pieces of a tree or trees that you have gathered from the ground, such as branches, leaves, needles, bark, etc. Lay these pieces on the center of the sheet for the toddlers to see. After the toddlers have seen all the pieces, invite them to examine the tree parts more carefully. Ask if they know what these items are part of.

On a sheet of paper taped to the wall or on an easel, draw a simple outline of a tree such as the one shown on page 41. Ask the toddlers to show you where the various parts fit on the tree. As the children show you, tape the parts to the tree outline. Ask, "Who gives us trees?" The answer: "God does."

Song
Ring Around God's Tree
Hold hands with the group and walk around in a circle. The group falls to floor on the last line. Chant to "Ring Around the Rosie."

Ring around God's tree
Hanging on the branches,
Leaves and needles
We all fall down!

Prayer
Trees Are Fun

Thank you, God, for giving us trees,
Branches moving in the breeze,
(*move arms like branches blowing in the wind*)
Leaves that reach for the sun,
(*stretch arms upward toward the sun*)
Trees are fun for everyone!
(*extend open arms*)

Finger Play
Five trees

There are five trees in the park,
(*hold up a hand with fingers spread*)
One is very small,
(*hold up just the pinky*)
One is very tall.
(*add the ring finger*)

One has apples that fall,
(*add the middle finger*)
One has a bird in a nest.
(*add the index finger*)
I like the old tree the best.
(*hold up just the thumb*)

Craft
Scribble a tree

Tape a few scraps of sandpaper onto a low table top. Tape down the edges of a sheet of paper over each of the pieces of sandpaper. Invite the toddlers to make the branches of a tree. Give each toddler a green nontoxic marker or crayon to scribble on one of the sheets of paper. After he or sheehas finished, untape his picture and help him or her add a trunk using a brown marker or crayon.

Scribble tree

Wrap-up

Can you see?

Finish class by going to the window and playing "Can you see…?" Start by shading your eyes with your hand and saying, "I see a tree. Can you see a tree?" Wait for their responses. Make sure all the toddlers who are looking for the item, find it.

I see a flower. Can you see the flower?

I see grass. Can you see grass?

(*If weather prohibits you from seeing these items, place pictures of the items around the room for searching fun.*)

End the activity by asking the children who made all of the wonderful plants, flowers, blades of grass, and trees? God did!

Sing the "Good-bye Song" or "Blessing Song" found on page 119.

Day Three of Creation
God Gives Us Trees

Today's Finger Play
Five Trees

There are five trees in the park,
(*hold up a hand with fingers spread*)
One is very small,
(*hold up just the pinky*)
One is very tall.
(*add the ring finger*)
One has apples that fall,
(*add the middle finger*)
One has a bird in a nest.
(*add the index finger*)
I like the old tree the best.
(*hold up just the thumb*)

Today in the Nursery
We played "ring around God's tree" and used sandpaper to make scribble trees. We did a finger-play about five trees and thanked God for giving us trees!

Family Activity
Play "Can you see…?" Sit in the yard or look out the window with your toddler and say, "I see a tree. Can you see a tree?" Wait for your toddler's response and then continue with flowers, grass, etc. When you are finished, gently fold your toddler's hands in yours and say, "Thank you God for loving us and giving us all the wonderful gifts of your creation."

Day Three of Creation
God Gives Us Trees

Today's Finger Play
Five Trees

There are five trees in the park,
(*hold up a hand with fingers spread*)
One is very small,
(*hold up just the pinky*)
One is very tall.
(*add the ring finger*)
One has apples that fall,
(*add the middle finger*)
One has a bird in a nest.
(*add the index finger*)
I like the old tree the best.
(*hold up just the thumb*)

Today in the Nursery
We played "ring around God's tree" and used sandpaper to make scribble trees. We did a finger-play about five trees and thanked God for giving us trees!

Family Activity
Play "Can you see…?" Sit in the yard or look out the window with your toddler and say, "I see a tree. Can you see a tree?" Wait for your toddler's response and then continue with flowers, grass, etc. When you are finished, gently fold your toddler's hands in yours and say, "Thank you God for loving us and giving us all the wonderful gifts of your creation."

Session Nine — Day Four of Creation
God Gives Us Sun

"Then God said: 'Let there be lights in the dome of the sky, to separate day from night. Let them mark the fixed times, the days and the years, and serve as luminaries in the dome of the sky, to shed light upon the earth.'"
Genesis 1:14-15

Dear Caregiver,

All of creation truly reflects the goodness and glory of God. The sun ushers in the morning and the warm rays shed God's light and love upon us. In this session the toddlers will explore some of the gifts God gives us through creation of the sun. They will make a beautiful "stained glass" to catch the sun's rays, watch what the warmth of the sun does to ice cubes, and make sun-rays dance through the room.

Session Options and Materials
❑ Ice-cube melting activity
  ✗ a tray of ice cubes or frozen fruit-juice cubes
  ✗ small paper or sipper-cups
❑ Five rays of sunshine finger-play
❑ Sun-ray dance
  ✗ yellow ribbon streamers
❑ Stained-glass craft
  ✗ clear contact paper
  ✗ scraps of bright cellophane gift-wrap

A Prayer for You
Creator of love and wisdom, as I share your wonderful creation with the toddlers, may I be a ray of love and light in their lives. Be present with us as we share your goodness and glory. Amen.

Day Four of Creation
God Gives Us Sun

Sing the "Hello Song" found on page 119.

Welcome

Ice-cube melt

Ahead of time, freeze an ice-cube tray of water or juice. As the toddlers come into the room, invite them to look at the tray of ice cubes. Place the tray in the direct warm sunlight. Tell the children to check the tray throughout their time together to see what happens.

Invite the toddlers to stand in the sun. Ask them how the sun makes them feel. You may need to give the toddlers some options such as happy, sad, warm, cold, etc. Tell the toddlers that God gives us the gift of sunshine. The sunshine helps the flowers and trees grow and makes us healthier and stronger, too.

If sunshine is not available in your nursery, substitute a reading lamp and place the ice cubes under the lamp in a dark-colored dish that will absorb the heat. You may also want to add a large paper sun on a wall.

Finger Play
Five Rays of Sunshine

Five rays of sunshine,
Made by God.
(*hold one hand up, wiggling all five fingers*)
One for the animals,
(*still holding hand up, point to one finger with
   each line*)
One for the trees,
One for the grass,
One for the flowers,
And one for me!

Prayer
Rays of Sunshine

Use the yellow ribbons as you sing this song to the tune of "Frère Jacques"

Rays of sunshine,
Rays of sunshine.
Sent by God,
Sent by God.
Helping all the grass grow,
Making us feel happy,
Thank you, God! Thank you, God!

Dance

Sun-ray

Give each toddler a twelve-inch strip of yellow ribbon. Tell the children that they are rays of God's sunshine. Play a tape of lively children's music and invite the toddlers to make their sun-ray (strip of ribbon) dance. Be sure you join in the fun.

Craft
Stained glass

Cut six-inch squares of clear contact-paper for each toddler. Put the squares on a low table, with the sticky side up and exposed. Give the toddlers scraps of bright cellophane gift-wrap or brightly colored tissue-paper to put on the sticky surface, making their own designs. When the toddler is finished, cover the sticky side with another piece of clear contact-paper. Hold the stained glass up for the toddler to look through. Send it home to be hung in a window as a reminder of the beautiful sunshine God gives us.

Stained-glass art

Wrap-up

Sun-melted drink

Gather the toddlers near the window where you left the ice cubes made of water or juice. Ask the toddlers to tell you how the ice melted. Carefully pour the water or juice from the ice-cube tray into a pitcher. Pour a small amount into a small paper or sipper-cup for each child to taste. Remind the toddlers that the sunshine not only helps flowers and trees to grow, but also makes us healthier and happier. End by saying "Thank you, God, for bright, happy days!"

Sing the "Good-bye Song" or "Blessing Song" found on page 119.

Day Four of Creation
God Gives Us Sun

Today in the Nursery
We made beautiful stained glass to hang up at home as a reminder of the sunshine God gives us to enjoy. We watched as the sun melted ice-cubes to provide a drink for us. We thanked God for making the sunshine to help the flowers and trees grow and make us healthier and stronger.

Family Activity
♥ Go out and play in the sunshine stopping to thank God for the beautiful, bright day.
♥ At family prayer time use a favorite picture-book to point to some of the things that need the sun to grow and be healthy, including people. End by doing today's finger play together.

Today's Finger Play
Five rays of sunshine
Five rays of sunshine,
Made by God.
(*hold one hand up, wiggling all five fingers*)
One for the animals,
(*still holding hand up, point to one finger with each line*)
One for the trees,
One for the grass,
One for the flowers,
And one for me!

Day Four of Creation
God Gives Us Sun

Today in the Nursery
We made beautiful stained glass to hang up at home as a reminder of the sunshine God gives us to enjoy. We watched as the sun melted ice-cubes to provide a drink for us. We thanked God for making the sunshine to help the flowers and trees grow and make us healthier and stronger.

Family Activity
♥ Go out and play in the sunshine stopping to thank God for the beautiful, bright day.
♥ At family prayer time use a favorite picture-book to point to some of the things that need the sun to grow and be healthy, including people. End by doing today's finger play together.

Today's Finger Play
Five rays of sunshine
Five rays of sunshine,
Made by God.
(*hold one hand up, wiggling all five fingers*)
One for the animals,
(*still holding hand up, point to one finger with each line*)
One for the trees,
One for the grass,
One for the flowers,
And one for me!

God Gives Us Stars and Moon

"And so it happened: God made the two great lights, the greater one to govern the day, and the lesser one to govern the night; and he made the stars. God set them in the dome of the sky, to shed light upon the earth, to govern the day and night, and to separate the light from darkness. God saw how good it was."

Genesis 1:15-18

Session Options and Materials
❑ Surprise-box activity
  ✗ star and moon shapes cut from Styrofoam trays or cardboard for each toddler
  ✗ a box with a cover
❑ "The Star" song
❑ **Good Night Moon** story-book
  ✗ the book **Good Night Moon** by Margaret Wise Brown
❑ Yarn-wrapped stars and moons craft
  ✗ multiple colors of yarn cut into twelve-inch pieces
  ✗ scotch tape
❑ Bedtime prayer
❑ Dancing stars and moons movement
❑ Copied family note for each child

Dear Caregiver,
God fashioned the universe as an extension of his heavenly reign. All that is, came into being by God's hand. When we look toward the sky on a beautiful evening and view the majestic heavens filled with dancing stars and a glowing moon, we see God's awesome power. The Lord God Almighty created heaven and earth. In this session, you will look to the sky once again with the toddlers. This time it will be the night sky. To celebrate God's majesty, the toddlers will make yarn-wrapped stars and moons, and pretend to be falling asleep as they see the stars and moons, aglow with God's love for them.

A Prayer for You
God, you are truly the Lord, Almighty, creator of heaven and earth. Thanks be to you for the beauty of our Universe. Be with us as we continue to explore creation and your tremendous love for us. Amen.

Day Four of Creation
God Gives Us Stars and Moon
Sing the "Hello Song" found on page 119.

Welcome

Surprise box

In preparation for this session, cut star and moon shapes on facing page out of Styrofoam trays or cardboard for every toddler in your group. Place them in a box with a cover. As your session begins, sit down in the middle of the floor with the box in front of you. Invite the toddlers over and tell them there is a surprise in the box. Ask them what they think it might be. After they have offered a few guesses, tell the toddlers that the box is very hard to get open unless you say "Abracadabra!" really loud as you wave your hand over it. Ask them to help you. After you have had fun opening the box, take out a star. Encourage them to tell you what it is, where they would find one, and what it does. Do the same for the moon. Reveal that there is a star and a moon in the box for everyone that they may do something with at craft time.

Song
The Star
Sing to the tune of "Twinkle, Twinkle Little Star." Invite the toddlers to hold their hands up high to make shining stars by wiggling their fingers while you sing.

Twinkle, twinkle little star;
Glowing with God's love for me.
Up above the world so high
God's great light is shining bright!
Twinkle, twinkle little star,
Glowing with God's love for me.

Prayer
Bedtime
Ask the toddlers what they do before they go to bed. Tell them that one very important thing to do is to talk to God. The prayer you are going to read to them is one they could use to talk to God. Invite them to pretend that they are falling asleep as you read this bedtime prayer to them.

The night has come,
It's time for bed.
I close my eyes as I rest my head.
Thank you, God, for this great day.
You know how much I like to play.
As you watch me from above,
I'll see your stars glow with love.
Amen.

Story

Good Night Moon
Read the book **Good Night Moon** by Margaret Wise Brown (Scholastic). This book can be found in the public library, if not in the children's section of your church library. As you read the book to the children, invite the toddlers to repeat each of the lines after you. As they look at the pictures ask the children questions about what is on the pages.

Craft
Yarn-wrapped star and moon shapes

Give each of the toddlers one moon- and one star-shape from the surprise box. Cut twelve-inch pieces of multiple color yarns. Invite each toddler to choose a piece of yarn to wrap around either his/her star- or moon-shape. Tape one end of the yarn on the shape and have the toddler wrap the yarn around it, making a textured design. Continue the process with additional pieces of yarn until the toddler is happy with his or her creation.

Wrap-up

Dancing stars and moons

(*Give each child his/her star and moon. Tell the toddlers to hide their creations behind their backs until they hear the name of each, then they should bring them out dancing.*)

When I see,
A dancing star and happy moon,
I know that bedtime is coming soon.
(*hide again the stars and moons behind their backs*)

God made
Dancing stars and a happy moon
To light up the night
As the wind whispers a good night tune.

Sing the "Good-bye Song" or "Blessing Song" found on page 119.

Day Four of Creation
God Gives Us Stars and Moon

Today's Prayer
Bedtime

The night has come,
It's time for bed.
I close my eyes as I rest my head.
Thank you, God, for this great day.
You know how much I like to play.
As you watch me from above,
I'll see your stars glow with love.
Amen.

Family Activity
♥ Hang the star and moon your toddler brings home in a place where the whole family will see them as a reminder of God's glowing love for each person.
♥ Just after dark and after your toddler has had a long nap, go out in the yard to look into the sky. Talk about the beauty of the sky and God's love shining down.

Today in the Nursery
We made yarn-wrapped stars and moons that danced through our room. Then we read a story called **Good Night Moon** about a child going to bed. At prayer time, we thanked God for making the stars and the moon that glow with God's love.

Day Four of Creation
God Gives Us Stars and Moon

Today's Prayer
Bedtime

The night has come,
It's time for bed.
I close my eyes as I rest my head.
Thank you, God, for this great day.
You know how much I like to play.
As you watch me from above,
I'll see your stars glow with love.
Amen.

Family Activity
♥ Hang the star and moon your toddler brings home in a place where the whole family will see them as a reminder of God's glowing love for each person.
♥ Just after dark and after your toddler has had a long nap, go out in the yard to look into the sky. Talk about the beauty of the sky and God's love shining down.

Today in the Nursery
We made yarn-wrapped stars and moons that danced through our room. Then we read a story called **Good Night Moon** about a child going to bed. At prayer time, we thanked God for making the stars and the moon that glow with God's love.

God Gives Us Fish, Frogs, and Turtles

"Then God said, 'Let the water teem with an abundance of living creatures…. And so it happened: God created the great sea monsters and all kinds of swimming creatures with which the water teems…. God saw how good it was and blessed them saying, 'Be fertile, multiply, and fill the water of the seas….' "
Genesis 1:20-22

Dear Caregiver,

God has filled the waters on earth with many species of sea life. Inviting toddlers to look closely at the many creatures God has placed in the sea will help them to discover how varied nature truly is. Sorting and classifying the sea-life pictures, mimicking their movements, and creating a sea-window collage are simple ways toddlers can celebrate the uniqueness of all God's creation this session.

Session Options and Materials
☐ Sea-life picture craft
   ✗ pictures of sea life (magazine, photograph, and /or coloring book)
   ✗ large, sturdy, empty box
   ✗ glue stick or paste
☐ "God Made Life in the Sea" finger-play
☐ Boat ride/sea-life movement
☐ Sea-life window collage
   ✗ paper plates, plastic wrap, tape, copies of day's prayer (optional: sand and seashells) (see page 55)
☐ "Big Fish, Little Fish" prayer
   ✗ one set for each child of cutout fish patterns (page 124) (red, blue, large, and small)
☐ Fishing activity
   ✗ materials to make fishing rods such as paper-towel tubes, string, magnets
   ✗ juice-can lids
☐ Copied family note for each child

A Prayer for You
God, creator of all life, I see the beauty of your creation in the life that flows from the seas. The waters of the earth are filled with such a variety of species. As I help to reveal this beauty to the toddlers, keep me attentive to the needs of each individual around me. Amen.

Day Five of Creation
God Gives Us Fish, Frogs, and Turtles
Sing the "Hello Song" found on page 119.

Welcome

Sea-life pictures
Before the children arrive, scatter pictures of fish, turtles, frogs, and seashells on the floor. In the midst of the pictures place a sturdy, large, empty, cardboard box. As the children arrive, encourage them to classify and sort the scattered pictures. Talk about how God has filled the water with a variety of sea life. Using a glue stick, help the children attach the pictures to the outside of the box.

Finger Play
God Made Life in the Sea

God made …
Fish swimming in the sea.
(move hand in a wavy motion)
Tutles sunning on the sand.
(cover a closed fist with an open hand)
And seashells that hide
(place closed fists together)
Something inside.
(open fists and wiggle fingers out)

Prayer
Big Fish, Little Fish
As you share the prayer with the toddlers, hold up a paper cutout to match the fish mentioned — a red fish, a blue fish, a big fish, and a little fish.

You fill the sea
With many fish for me.
Some are red, some are blue.
Big fish, little fish,
God, I thank you. Amen.

Movement

Boat ride/sea life
Place a few children in the box and push the box around the room, pretending to be a boat sailing in the sea. (Depending on the number of children you may want to have more than one box available.) As you give the rides say this rhyme to the children. Teach an action for each of the animals mentioned. Encourage the children to imitate the actions as you say the rhyme.

Tote and float
The kids in our boat
What did God put in the sea?
Frogs that jump, fish that flap,
And turtles that snap.
All this for you and me!

Craft
Sea-life window

Give toddlers a blue crayon or nontoxic marker to decorate a paper plate. Then from a bowl or other container allow the toddlers to select fish cutouts to place on the plate. (Optional: Add a pinch of sand and seashells.) Cover the plate with plastic wrap and tape lightly in place. On the under side of the paper-plate glue or tape the day's prayer for each child to share at home. Use the fish patterns on page 124.

Wrap-up

Fishing

Using paper-towel tubes, string, and magnets, make pretend fishing poles. Using the fishing poles with the children to pick up different, metal juice-can lids. Stickers depicting sea life may be placed on one side of the lids to add to the fun. Older toddlers will enjoy making this a matching game, while younger toddlers will find a challenge in attaching the magnet "hook" to the metal lids. As the toddlers catch these, ask the children "What did God put in the sea?" Continue to remind the children what a wonderful world God has made.

Sing the "Good-bye Song" or "Blessing Song" found on page 119.

Day Five of Creation
God Gives Us Fish, Frogs, and Turtles

Today's Finger Play
*God made life in the sea
God made…
Fish swimming in the sea.*
(*move hand in a wavy motion*)
Turtles sunning on the sand.
(*cover a closed fist with an open hand*)
And seashells that hide
(*place closed fists together*)
Something inside.
(*open fists and wiggle fingers out*)

Family Activity
Visit sea life at a local zoo, aquarium, or pet store. As you and your toddler describe all the different colors and kinds of sea life you see, take time to thank God for all the variety we find in the world.

Today in the Nursery
We talked about all the life God has placed in the sea. We have so many water creatures to be thankful for, fish, frogs, turtles, even seashells. We made a fish picture with a prayer on the back that we want to share with you.

Day Five of Creation
God Gives Us Fish, Frogs, and Turtles

Today's Finger Play
*God made life in the sea
God made…
Fish swimming in the sea.*
(*move hand in a wavy motion*)
Turtles sunning on the sand.
(*cover a closed fist with an open hand*)
And seashells that hide
(*place closed fists together*)
Something inside.
(*open fists and wiggle fingers out*)

Family Activity
Visit sea life at a local zoo, aquarium, or pet store. As you and your toddler describe all the different colors and kinds of sea life you see, take time to thank God for all the variety we find in the world.

Today in the Nursery
We talked about all the life God has placed in the sea. We have so many water creatures to be thankful for, fish, frogs, turtles, even seashells. We made a fish picture with a prayer on the back that we want to share with you.

Session Twelve — Day Five of Creation
God Gives Us Birds

"Then God said, '… on the earth let birds fly beneath the dome of the sky.' And so it happened: God created … all kinds of winged birds. God saw how good it was, and God blessed them, saying '… let the birds multiply on the earth.' "
Genesis 1:20-22

Dear Caregiver,

Watching the sky as birds fly by and listening to them chirp early in the morning are everyday reminders that God has filled our world with nature's wonder. Seeing a bird pull up a worm or quietly watching as a mother bird builds a nest reminds us that God does provide. This session gives the toddlers the opportunities to imitate a few of these bird actions, while praising and thanking God for these winged creations.

Session Options and Materials
❑ Bird-nest blanket ride activity
  ✗ a blanket
  ✗ a picture of a bird nest
❑ "Ten Little Birds" action song
❑ "Blessed Busy Birds" flannel-board story
  ✗ flannel-board patterns
  ✗ flannel board
❑ Pocket-nest craft
  ✗ marker
  ✗ paper plates
  ✗ scissors and hole punch for adult use
  ✗ nesting fill (straw, yarn, or Easter grass)
  ✗ extra cutouts of flannel-board patterns
❑ "Birds Flying Above" prayer
❑ Hide-and-seek bird game
❑ Copied family note for each child

A Prayer for You
Dear Lord, as a bird's flight is directed by the wind, please direct our journey closer to you by surrounding us with the Holy Spirit. Send your Spirit to guide us as we present your splendor to these eager toddlers. Amen.

Day Five of Creation
God Gives Us Birds
Sing the "Hello Song" found on page 119.

Welcome

Blanket ride

Use a blanket to give the toddlers blanket rides. Children sit on the blanket as an adult pulls the blanket around the room. After the children (or the adult) tire from this play, sit on the blanket for a rest. If available, show the children a bird nest, or a picture of one. Talk about how God made birds to fly and sing. Look out a window to find a bird flying. Listen for birds chirping and singing outside. Pretend with the toddlers:
- ✔ to rest in a nest (the blanket).
- ✔ to fly from the nest flapping their arms.
- ✔ to chirp and tweet like birds.

Song Finger-Play
Ten Little Birdies
Sing to the tune of "Ten Little Indians," wiggling a finger for each bird.

> One little, two little,
> Three little birdies.
> Four little, five little,
> Six little birdies.
> Seven little, eight little,
> Nine little birdies,
> Ten little birdies that fly.
> (*hook thumbs together and wave hands
>   up high in a flying motion*)

Prayer
Birds Flying Above
Encourage the toddlers to stand in place and gently flap their arms as you say this prayer.

> God, when I see the
> Birds flying above,
> Each day I will know
> That I am loved. Amen.

Story

Blessed Busy Birds

Make into a flannel board or act out with movement, using the patterns on the facing page

Green bird flies high to a tree
To see what he can see.
Muddy bird takes a splish-splash
And flies off in a dash.
And they sing "God made me!"
(*have the children echo this quote back*)

Mother bird makes a soft nest
So her babies can rest.
Hungry bird digs for a worm
And watches it squirm.
And they sing, "We are blessed!"
(*have the children echo this quote back*)

Craft
Pocket nest

Cut a paper plate in half for each child. Place the half-plate face-down over a full plate. Staple the edges together to form a pocket. Give the toddlers a plate-pocket to fill with straw, yarn, or Easter grass. Above the pocket nest, using the child's name, print "_____ is blessed!" Provide copies of the bird pattern below for the children to color and place in the pocket nest. Punch two holes at the top and thread a ribbon to make a hanger. Send the pocket nest home to remind families how blessed they are.

Wrap-up

Hide-and-seek bird

While waiting for families to arrive, play a game of hide-and-seek. Hide the bird patterns used for the story in very obvious places. As the children find them, encourage the toddlers to return the paper birds back to the nest (blanket). When all the birds are back together and safe in their nest, play again and let the toddlers hide the birds.

Sing the "Good-bye Song" or "Blessing Song" found on page 119.

Day Five of Creation
God Gives Us Birds

Today's Finger Play
Ten Little Birdies
Sing to the tune of "Ten Little Indians,"
wiggling a finger for each bird.
>One little, two little,
>Three little birdies.
>Four little, five little,
>Six little birdies.
>Seven little, eight little,
>Nine little birdies,
>Ten little birdies that fly.
>(*hook thumbs together and*
>   *wave hands up high in a flying motion*)

Family Activity
♥ While outside with your toddler look for birds flying and listen for birds singing and chirping. When you notice the birds, point to the bird and whisper to your toddler "God blesses birds and God blesses us!"
♥ Look for a bird nest to show your toddler and talk about how we care for all of God's blessings.

Today in the Nursery
We pretended to be birds that fly and chirp. We went for blanket rides and rested in a nest. We talked about how God blesses the birds and God blesses us.

Day Five of Creation
God Gives Us Birds

Today's Finger Play
Ten Little Birdies
Sing to the tune of "Ten Little Indians,"
wiggling a finger for each bird.
>One little, two little,
>Three little birdies.
>Four little, five little,
>Six little birdies.
>Seven little, eight little,
>Nine little birdies,
>Ten little birdies that fly.
>(*hook thumbs together and*
>   *wave hands up high in a flying motion*)

Family Activity
♥ While outside with your toddler look for birds flying and listen for birds singing and chirping. When you notice the birds, point to the bird and whisper to your toddler "God blesses birds and God blesses us!"
♥ Look for a bird nest to show your toddler and talk about how we care for all of God's blessings.

Today in the Nursery
We pretended to be birds that fly and chirp. We went for blanket rides and rested in a nest. We talked about how God blesses the birds and God blesses us.

Session Thirteen — Day Six of Creation
God Gives Us Animals

"Then God said, 'Let the earth bring forth all kinds of living creatures: cattle, creeping things, and wild animals of all kinds.' And so it happened: God made all kinds of wild animals, all kinds of cattle, and all kinds of creeping things on the earth. God saw how good it was."
Genesis 1:24-25

Dear Caregiver,

God makes the animals, all sizes, shapes, and colors. Young children are drawn to animals and very often find them among their best friends. Toddlers carry on conversations with worms, puppies, and teddy bears. Animals are intriguing for children to watch, learn about, and imitate. In this session the toddlers will discover that God made the animals, have fun with a kitten named Mitten and a puppy named Toughy, learn the names and sounds of a variety of animals, and say a thank-you prayer for the gift of animals.

Session Options and Materials
❑ Surprise-tote game
  ✗ canvas or paper bag containing a stuffed animal
❑ Animal sounds activity
  ✗ "Old MacDonald Had a Farm" song (modified to fit this session)
❑ "A Kitten Named Mitten" rhyme
  ✗ puppet patterns
  ✗ kitten
  ✗ puppy
  ✗ 5½-by-8½-inch gray or white construction paper (for kitten)
  ✗ 5½-by-8½-inch black or brown construction paper (for puppy)
  ✗ crayons (optional)
❑ "Thank You, God, For Animals" prayer
❑ Animal walk-and-talk movement
  a basket- or box-full of stuffed animals
❑ Copied family note for each child
• To prepare for Session Fourteen's craft you need to take each child's photo today.

A Prayer for You
"Praise the Lord ... You wild beasts and all tame animals, you creeping things and you winged fowl" (Psalm 148:7, 10). God, creator of all living things, be with me as I share the wonder and delight of your creation with the children. Amen.

Day Six of Creation
God Gives Us Animals
Sing the "Hello Song" found on page 119.

Welcome

Surprise tote

As the children arrive, gently shake the bag with the stuffed animal inside. Make sounds and manipulate the bag so that the children are wondering if the object in your bag is alive. Ask them what they think is in your bag. Slowly pull the stuffed animal out until they are able to guess the name of the stuffed animal. Ask the children what sound the animal would make, where the animal would live, etc. Tell the toddlers, "God made this animal and all the other animals."

Song
Old MacDonald Had a Farm
Sing "Old MacDonald Had a Farm" with the children making the following changes.

Old MacDonald had a farm, E-I-E-I-O
And on his farm God made a pig, E-I-E-I-O
With an oink-oink here, and an oink-oink there,
Here an oink, there an oink, everywhere an oink-oink.
Old MacDonald had a farm and God made his pig.

As you add other animals and sounds, remember to also add hand movements showing twitching ears, swishing tails, waving paws, etc. with sounds.

Prayer
Animals I Meet
Have the children repeat each phrase and make the animal sounds.

Thank you, God, for cows that say moo, moo
And chicks that say peep, peep.
Help me to be kind to the animals I meet. Amen.

Activity
Animal sounds

Gather several stuffed animals in a basket. As you pull one animal out at a time say, "God made the _____. What does the _____ say to you?" Allow the toddlers to play with the basket of animals. Encourage the toddlers to take turns and share.

Craft
A Kitten Named Mitten

Copy the puppy and kitten patterns on to the 5½-by-8½-inch construction paper or tag board. Cut out the puppet figures and the two finger-holes in each. Use the finger puppets to tell the following rhyme. Be sure to put the name of each child on the back of his or her puppets. The toddlers could add more color to each with crayons.

I know a kitten named Mitten,
Who plays with a puppy named Toughy.
God made them, as cute as can be,
They are good friends for you and me.

Wrap-up

Animal walk and talk

Using the basket of animals invite the toddlers, one at a time, to choose an animal. The same animal may be chosen over and over again. Tell the toddlers that this time you are going to imitate the movement and sound of the animal chosen. Encourage the toddlers to help you.

Sing the "Good-bye Song" or "Blessing Song" found on page 119.

Day Six of Creation
God Gives Us Animals

Today in the Nursery

We talked about God making all of the animals. Our finger puppets Mitten and Toughy helped us to tell the rhyme.

Today's Finger-puppet Rhyme

I know a kitten named Mitten,
Who plays with a puppy named Toughy.
God made them, as cute as can be,
They are good friends for you and me.

Family Activity

♥ Talk about the animals your family sees, what they look like, what sounds they make, and where they live.

♥ Gather all the animals in your house, stuffed or real, and say this short prayer of thanksgiving:

Thank you, God, for cows that say moo, moo
And chicks that say peep, peep.
Help me to be kind to the animals I meet.

Day Six of Creation
God Gives Us Animals

Today in the Nursery

We talked about God making all of the animals. Our finger puppets Mitten and Toughy helped us to tell the rhyme.

Today's Finger-puppet Rhyme

I know a kitten named Mitten,
Who plays with a puppy named Toughy.
God made them, as cute as can be,
They are good friends for you and me.

Family Activity

♥ Talk about the animals your family sees, what they look like, what sounds they make, and where they live.

♥ Gather all the animals in your house, stuffed or real, and say this short prayer of thanksgiving:

Thank you, God, for cows that say moo, moo
And chicks that say peep, peep.
Help me to be kind to the animals I meet.

Session Fourteen — Day Six of Creation
God Creates People

"Then God said, 'Let us make man in our image, after our likeness. Let them have dominion over the fish of the sea, the birds of the air, and the cattle, and over all the wild animals and all the creatures that crawl on the ground.' God created man in his image; in the divine image he created him; male and female he created them. God blessed them, saying: 'Be fertile and multiply; fill the earth and subdue it. Have dominion over the fish of the sea, the birds of the air, and all the living things that move on the earth.' "

Genesis 1:26-28

Dear Caregiver,

What an awesome place God has given humankind in creation. Not only are we made in God's divine image, but we have also been made stewards of creation. God must truly love us, for we are called to enjoy and care for all the wonderful treasures God has given us.

Every toddler in the nursery is a holy, precious, and unique gift of God's love. It is important for children to hear how much God loves them and how extraordinary each of them is. In this session, the toddlers will hear that God made each one in a very special way and that God loves them very much.

Session Options and Materials
- ❑ Body identification game
- ❑ "Head and Shoulders" action song
- ❑ "Big Red Ball" story
    - ✗ a large plastic or rubber ball
- ❑ Magnet picture craft
    - ✗ an instant camera and film
    - ✗ one juice-can lid per child
    - ✗ glue
    - ✗ magnet strip
- ❑ "Thank you, God, For Making Me" prayer
- ❑ Rolling-the-ball activity
    - ✗ a flat double-size sheet
- ❑ Copied family note for each child

A Prayer for You

God of love, I am called by you to share my faith with these young children. Help me to appreciate the unique and precious gift of love that each one of them has. Let me be a reflection of your unending and compassionate love for every one of these toddlers. Amen.

Day Six of Creation
God Creates People
Sing the "Hello Song" found on page 119.

Welcome

Body identification

   Sit down on the floor near the toddlers. Touch your nose, saying to the children, "I am touching my nose. Can you touch your nose?" Continue the fun with other parts — hands, ears, feet, etc. Then use maybe less-familiar words such as elbow, chin, ankles. Tell the children that everyone of them is very special. Ask them, "Who made you each so very special?" God did!

Song
Head and Shoulders
Sing to the tune of "London Bridge Is Falling Down"

   Head and shoulders,
   Knees and toes,
   Knees and toes,
   Knees and toes.
   Head and shoulders,
   Knees and toes,
   My God made me!

Prayer
Thank You, God, for Making Me

   Thank you, God, for
   Making me.
   (*point to self*)
   With eyes to see and
   Ears to hear,
   (*point to eyes, then ears*)
   With a mouth to smile
   And hands that catch,
   (*point to mouth, hold hands out*)
   I am so happy to be me!
   Thank you God for
   Making me!
   (*hug self*)

Story

Big Red Ball
   Use a large plastic or rubber ball to help tell this story.
   I see a ball, it's very big and bright red. The ball goes high above my head. (*Move ball above head.*)
   I want to catch that big red ball. I run with my feet. (*Run in place.*) I reach out with my arms and hands (*stretch out arms in a reaching motion*) so I can catch that big red ball! (*Throw the ball up in the air and catch it.*)
   I'm so happy that God gave me feet, arms, and hands so that I can catch the big red ball! (*Point to body parts as named.*)
   God loves me very much! (*Give yourself a hug.*)

Craft
Magnet picture
Use an instant camera, or pictures taken and developed the week before. Show each of the children his or her picture. Tell the children that no two people look exactly the same. God made each one of them a little bit different. That makes each of them very special. Glue snapshots or a photocopy of the children onto the juice-can lids. Glue magnets on the back of the lids. Send them home for the family's refrigerator.

Magnet picture

Wrap-up

Rolling the ball
Invite the toddlers to sit around the edge of a flat, double-size sheet. Roll the ball to one of the toddlers asking them to continue to roll the ball to each other as you chant:

Roll the ball with two hands,
With two hands, with two hands,
Roll the ball with two hands
To all our friends.

Continue the play using other phrases one hand, one leg, two legs etc.

Sing the "Good-bye Song" or "Blessing Song" found on page 119.

Day Six of Creation
God Creates People

Today's Song
Head and Shoulders
Sing to the tune of "London Bridge Is Falling Down"

Head and shoulders,
Knees and toes,
Knees and toes,
Knees and toes.
Head and shoulders,
Knees and toes,
My God made me!

Today in the Nursery
We made picture magnets to help us remember that God made each of us to be very special!

Family Activity
During prayer time at home, touch your nose and say, "Thank you, God, for my nose." Encourage your toddler to do the same. Continue with other body parts. End by saying, "Thank you, God, for making each of us so special."

♥ Glue pictures of family members onto juice-can lids. Glue magnets on the backs of the lids. Your toddler will enjoy hours of fun arranging them.

♥ Remind your toddler often that God loves him/her very much!

Day Six of Creation
God Creates People

Today's Song
Head and Shoulders
Sing to the tune of "London Bridge Is Falling Down"

Head and shoulders,
Knees and toes,
Knees and toes,
Knees and toes.
Head and shoulders,
Knees and toes,
My God made me!

Today in the Nursery
We made picture magnets to help us remember that God made each of us to be very special!

Family Activity
During prayer time at home, touch your nose and say, "Thank you, God, for my nose." Encourage your toddler to do the same. Continue with other body parts. End by saying, "Thank you, God, for making each of us so special."

♥ Glue pictures of family members onto juice-can lids. Glue magnets on the backs of the lids. Your toddler will enjoy hours of fun arranging them.

♥ Remind your toddler often that God loves him/her very much!

God Rested

"Thus the heavens and the earth and all their array were completed. Since on the seventh day God was finished with the work he had been doing, he rested on the seventh day from all the work he had undertaken."
Genesis 2:1-2

Session Options and Materials
❑ Resting-corner activity
  ✗ rest-time objects such as a pillow, blanket or sleeping bag, sheet, story book, puzzles, stuffed animals
❑ "Are You Resting?" song
❑ "Romping and Resting" action story
❑ Tie-dyed art
  ✗ one copy of the rest-time pattern on page 71 for each toddler, on stiff paper
  ✗ one coffee-filter per toddler
  ✗ permanent marker
  ✗ three colors of food coloring
  ✗ bowls and water
  ✗ newspapers
❑ "Rest and Play" prayer
❑ Romp-and-rest game
❑ Copied family note for each child

Dear Caregiver,
Thus the heavens and the earth were completed and filled with life. Then God, the creator of heaven and earth, rested. Between the ordered creation and the creator, a special relationship is set up. Shaped into all that God created is the tendency toward goodness and growth, which leads to rest in God alone. The toddler's experience of rest is a break from the action, a time to be quiet and restore one's energy. In this session the toddlers will set up a "resting" corner and play "romp and rest" as they explore God's creation.

A Prayer for You
God in whom we find rest, you not only created the universe but renew it by the power of your Holy Spirit. Renew me, Lord, through community, worship, prayer, and rest in you. Help me to remember that the nursery is a holy place where your renewing love is shared. Amen.

Day Seven of Creation
God Rested

Sing the "Hello Song" found on page 119.

Welcome

Resting corner

Lay out items a toddler may use during a rest time such as a pillow, blanket, teddy bear, and storybook. Invite the toddlers to gather around you. Ask them, "What do you think you might do with these things?" Then ask if they have a rest- or nap-time at home when they get tired. With their help, set up a rest corner complete with a couple of blankets and/or sleeping bags, storybooks, etc. If possible set it up in a corner where you can hang a sheet overhead. Tell the toddlers that after God finished making all the wonderful things in the world, God saw that it was good and God rested. Invite the toddlers to go to the rest corner to look at books or play quietly wherever they wish.

Song
Are You Resting?

As you sing this song, invite the toddlers to pretend they are getting sleepy, stretch, yawn, and slowly fall to sleep.
(sing to the tune of "Frère Jacques")

Are you resting?
Are you resting?
Little friends, little friends,
God is with you as you rest,
God is with you as you rest,
Little friends, little friends.

Prayer
Rest and Play

Hello God,
I can run, hop and jump all day.
(*run in place, hop, jump*)
Then I can crawl into my bed,
and lay down my weary head.
(*place head on folded hands*)
Thanks, God, for rest and play!

Action Story

Romping and resting

*Tell toddlers that you are going to tell them a story about a very special group of children. Go on to say that you will need their help to tell the story. Ask them to listen very carefully and do the actions (in **bold italics**) with you that the children do in the story.*

One beautiful morning, a group of children went out to play. First they decided *to **hop like bunnies**. Then they **jumped like frogs**. After that they **swam like fish** and **crawled like turtles**. They **stretched and yawned** as they started to get tired, but they kept playing. The children **waddled like ducks** and **swayed like elephants**. "It is time to rest," the moms and dads called. The children were happy because they were so tired. They all went home and **curled up** on their soft beds for a good rest.

Craft
Tie-dyed pictures

Make a copy of the bedtime pattern on this page (can be used same-size or enlarged) for each toddler on stiff paper. Cover your work area with newspapers. Write each child's name on a coffee filter with a permanent marker. Help the toddlers fold the filters any way they would like until there is a piece about three inches in size. Next, have the children dip the folded filters into the bowls of water colored with food coloring. Let the colors run together. Help the toddlers squeeze out the excess water and then unfold their creations. Allow them to dry near a fan or heat vent.

Wrap-up

Romp and rest

Play "romp and rest" with the toddlers. Tell the toddlers that you are going to lead them in some fun activities such as the ones in today's story, but when you say the word "rest" the toddlers should pretend to fall asleep. You will have to model this for them as you play the game.

Lead them in two or three of these fun activities: Stretch like a cat, hop like a frog, waddle like a duck.

Then say, "Rest!" and pretend to fall asleep. At the end, remind them that after God finished making all the things in this beautiful world, God saw that they were good and God rested, too!

Sing the "Good-bye Song" or "Blessing Song" found on page 119.

- -

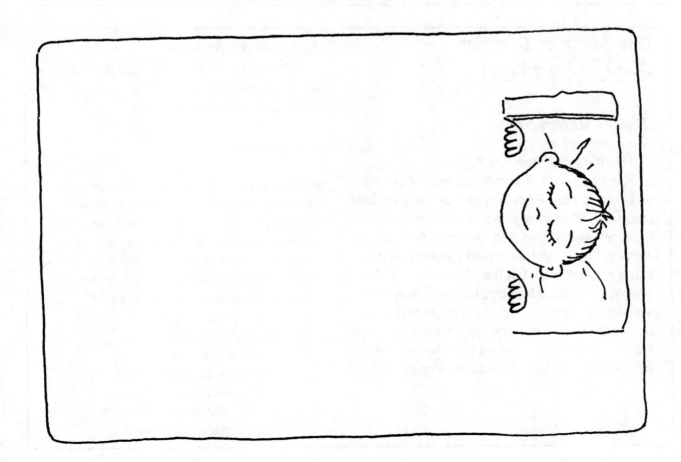

Day Seven of Creation
God Rested

Today's Action Story
Romping and resting

Do the **bold, italicized** actions.

One beautiful morning, a group of children went out to play. First they decided to **hop like bunnies**. Then they **jumped like frogs**. After that they **swam like fish** and **crawled like turtles**. They **stretched and yawned** as they started to get tired, but they kept playing. The children **waddled like ducks** and **swayed like elephants**. "It is time to rest," the moms and dads called. The children were happy because they were so tired. They all went home and **curled up** on their soft beds for a good rest.

Today in the Nursery
We set up a rest corner and played a game of "romping and resting." We thanked God for rest and play.

Family Activity

♥ Create a rest corner at home with your toddler. Use a favorite blanket, pillow, puzzle, and storybook. Encourage your toddler to go there whenever he or she feels tired and needs a rest. When your toddler is tired, sing this song to him. Sing to the tune of "Frère Jacques."

Are You Resting?
Are you resting?
Are you resting?
Little friends, little friends,
God is with you as you rest,
God is with you as you rest,
Little friends, little friends.

Day Seven of Creation
God Rested

Today's Action Story
Romping and resting

Do the **bold, italicized** actions.

One beautiful morning, a group of children went out to play. First they decided to **hop like bunnies**. Then they **jumped like frogs**. After that they **swam like fish** and **crawled like turtles**. They **stretched and yawned** as they started to get tired, but they kept playing. The children **waddled like ducks** and **swayed like elephants**. "It is time to rest," the moms and dads called. The children were happy because they were so tired. They all went home and **curled up** on their soft beds for a good rest.

Today in the Nursery
We set up a rest corner and played a game of "romping and resting." We thanked God for rest and play.

Family Activity

♥ Create a rest corner at home with your toddler. Use a favorite blanket, pillow, puzzle, and storybook. Encourage your toddler to go there whenever he or she feels tired and needs a rest. When your toddler is tired, sing this song to him. Sing to the tune of "Frère Jacques."

Are You Resting?
Are you resting?
Are you resting?
Little friends, little friends,
God is with you as you rest,
God is with you as you rest,
Little friends, little friends.

Session Sixteen — Day Seven of Creation
God Blessed the Seventh Day and Made It Holy

"So God blessed the seventh day and made it holy, because on it he rested from all the work he had done in creation."
Genesis 2:3

Dear Caregiver,

The special relationship with God's people is expressed in the blessing of the seventh day and in making it holy. Blessings express God's generosity and steadfast love for God's people. Making the day holy sets it apart for worship and religious activity. The early Christians began to celebrate the first day of the week because the Resurrection and the coming of the Holy Spirit at Pentecost had taken place on the first day. Introduce the toddlers to blessings as an expression of God's love for them. The toddlers are experiencing holy days in the nursery as they come together to play, to hear about God's great love for them, and to worship through song and prayer.

Session Options and Materials

❑ Build a church activity
  ✗ building blocks
  ✗ little toy people
❑ "This Is the Day We Go to Church" song
❑ "My church" art
  ✗ copy of patterns A and B on page 75 on stiff paper for each toddler
  ✗ pair of adult scissors
  ✗ glue, glue-stick or paste
  ✗ crayons or markers
❑ "Here Is the Church" action rhyme
❑ Wrap-up blessing prayer
  ✗ clean spray-bottle filled with water
❑ Copied family note for each child

A Prayer for You

God, bless me as I prepare to share your goodness on this holy day. Bless the toddlers, too, that they may feel your presence, and the love and joy of the community of faith surrounding them. Amen.

Day Seven of Creation

God Blessed the Seventh Day and Made It Holy

Sing the "Hello Song" found on page 119.

Welcome

Build a church

Collect all the blocks and other toy building items you have in the nursery. Also, gather any little toy people you have, such as round Duplo people. Invite the children to tell you about going to church. You may be surprised at their responses. Explain that God blessed creation when God was finished and made the day holy, or special. We keep the day holy when we come to church on Sunday with our friends to celebrate God's love for us and to learn more about God. Ask the children to help you build a church with the building materials. The toddlers will most likely build individual buildings. Pull all the creations together and put any little people you have inside the structure. Explain to the toddlers that at church people come together to give thanks and praise to God who loves us. Tell them that church is a very special and good place to be.

Song
This Is the Day We Go to Church

Sing to the tune of "Here We Go 'Round the Mulberry Bush" while walking in place or leading the group around the room.

> This is the way we go to church,
> We go to church,
> We go to church.
> This is the way we go to church,
> On Sunday morning.
> Additional verses:
> This is the way we pray in church
> (*fold your hands*)
> This is the way we shake hands
> (*shake hands*)
> This is the way we sing in church
> (*cup hands around mouth*)

Rhyme
Here Is the Church

Use the "My church" creations made by the toddlers with this traditional rhyme.

> Here is the church,
> (*hold up the church*)
> Here is the steeple,
> (*point to the steeple*)
> Open the doors,
> (*open the doors*)
> And see all the people.
> (*point to all the people*)

Craft
My church

Make a copy of pattern A (inside of the church) and pattern B (outside of the church) on stiff paper for each toddler. Cut pattern B on the dotted lines to make the doors open. Help the toddlers glue the outside of the church over the inside so when the doors open, the toddler will see all the people. Allow the toddlers to add color with crayons.

Wrap-up

Blessing prayer

Tell the toddlers again that God blessed the day to make it holy. God blesses us too. God's blessing reminds us that God loves us very much.

Sing the following blessing song to the toddlers. Using a clean spray-bottle, give each toddler a gentle spray of water whenever you sing "squirt" as a concrete sign of the blessing. You may want to gently spray hands. Sing the song over and over until all the toddlers who would like a little spray of water have had it.

(*Sing to the tune of "This Old Man."*)

God bless you, God bless me
God bless everyone you see.

With a squirt for you and a squirt for me
God loves us throughout the day.

Sing the "Good-bye Song" or "Blessing Song" found on page 119.

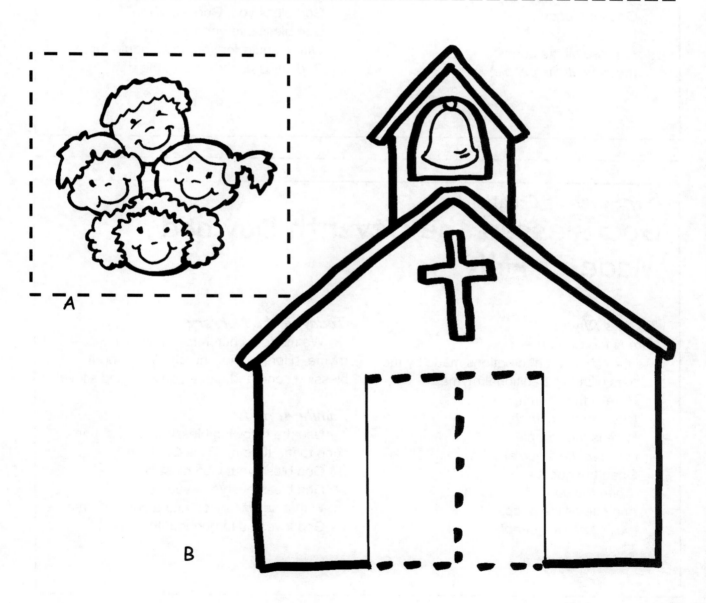

A

B

Day Seven of Creation

God Blessed the Seventh Day and Made It Holy

Today's Rhyme
Here Is the Church
Use the "My church" creations made by the toddlers with this traditional rhyme.

Here is the church,
(*hold up the church*)
Here is the steeple,
(*point to the steeple*)
Open the doors,
(*open the doors*)
And see all the people.
(*point to all the people*)

Today in the Nursery
We made a church to use with the rhyme, "Here Is the Church." We sang a blessing song and had a squirt of God's love!

Family Activity
Use the following blessing song at home, sung to the tune of "This Old Man."

God bless you, God bless me
God bless everyone you see.
With a squirt for you and a squirt for me
God loves us throughout the day.

Day Seven of Creation

God Blessed the Seventh Day and Made It Holy

Today's Rhyme
Here Is the Church
Use the "My church" creations made by the toddlers with this traditional rhyme.

Here is the church,
(*hold up the church*)
Here is the steeple,
(*point to the steeple*)
Open the doors,
(*open the doors*)
And see all the people.
(*point to all the people*)

Today in the Nursery
We made a church to use with the rhyme, "Here Is the Church." We sang a blessing song and had a squirt of God's love!

Family Activity
Use the following blessing song at home, sung to the tune of "This Old Man."

God bless you, God bless me
God bless everyone you see.
With a squirt for you and a squirt for me
God loves us throughout the day.

Joining Hands in Thanksgiving

"It is good to give thanks to the LORD, to sing praise to your name, Most High … For you make me glad, O LORD, by your deeds; at the works of your hands I rejoice."
Psalm 92:2, 5

Dear Caregiver,

Thanksgiving traditionally is a holiday when we gather around a meal with family and friends to give thanks to God for our many blessings. Toddlers, too, can enjoy the gathering for a meal and praising God for the many blessings bestowed upon each of us. But for toddlers, this holiday meal may seem no different from that of a simple dinner or breakfast with a few more people. Celebrate Thanksgiving with the toddlers by joining hands, gathering together, and singing out God's praise.

Session Options and Materials
❑ Sharing mealtime activity
  ✗ tablecloth
  ✗ child-safe (or toy) cups, plates, and other eating utensils
❑ "Gather 'Round" action song
❑ "Praise God" movement story
❑ Thank-you prayer
❑ Praying hands centerpiece craft
  ✗ colored construction paper
  ✗ glue or paste
  ✗ small dessert paper plate for each child
  ✗ a marker and scissors for adult use
❑ Hand group-collage
  ✗ large poster-board
❑ Copied family note for each child

A Prayer for You
God, there is so much to be thankful for: family, friends, and food. As I reach out my hands to help these children join in singing your praise, continue to nourish my faith, family, friends, and food. Amen.

Celebrating Thanksgiving
Joining Hands in Thanksgiving
Sing the "Hello Song" found on page 119.

Welcome

Sharing mealtime
Before the children arrive, spread a tablecloth in an open space. As the children arrive, ask them to bring any dishes, cups, pitchers, or other eating utensils that may be a part of your play toys. Sit down with the children and pretend to have a meal together. Encourage the children to get involved by offering them some pretend foods and drinks, or asking that they pass you a pretend food, etc. As you involve the children in this activity, discuss how families share mealtimes together.

Song
Gather 'Round
While holding hands and moving in a circle, sing to the tune of "Frère Jacques." On the last line of the song sit down and act out the action stated.

> Friends and family,
> Friends and family.
> Gather 'round,
> Gather 'round.
> We join hands together,
> We join hands together.
> At a meal, at a meal.

For more verses replace the last line: When we pray, While we play, Thanking God.

Prayer
Thank You
Encourage the toddlers to hold hands as you say this prayer.

> God, we join our hands to say, "Thank you for family, food, and friends." Amen.

Story

Praise God
Act out the actions with the toddlers as you retell this story. When you say "to praise God," lift hands high over head and shake them.

> We touch our toes to praise God.
> We clap our hands to praise God.
> We stretch our arms to praise God.
> We jump up and down to praise God.
> We make big circles (*using arms*) to praise God.
> We do the twist (*from side to side*) to praise God.
> We join our hands together to praise God.
> (*keeping hands together lift high*) A-MEN!
> (*bring hands down together*)

Craft
Praying hands

Trace each child's hand on construction paper. Cut out a pair of the hands, making sure to leave an extra length of paper at the wrist, as shown. With a drop of glue or paste, connect the fingertips. Mount the praying hands onto the underside of the paper plate at the wrist of the hands. With a marker write the message, "Today we thank God for …" around the edge of the plate. Send these centerpieces home with the families as a reminder to pray together in thanksgiving.

Praying hands

Wrap-up

Hand collage

On a large poster board write:

Thanksgiving
Friends and family
Join hands together
To thank God.

Using a pencil, trace each child's hand on the poster. Print the child's name on his/her hand and go over the pencil tracing using the marker. Hang the poster where the families will see it as they arrive to pick up their child.

Sing the "Good-bye Song" or "Blessing Song" found on page 119.

Celebrating Thanksgiving
Joining Hands in Thanksgiving

Today's Song
Gather 'Round
Sing to the tune of "Frère Jacques."
   Friends and family,
   Friends and family.
   Gather 'round,
   Gather 'round.
   We join hands together,
   We join hands together.
   At a meal, at a meal.
For more verses replace the last line:
When we pray, While we play, Thanking God.

Today in the Nursery
   We joined hands and thanked God in many ways for family, food, and friends. We played a game and we exercised while praising God.

Family Activity
♥ As you prepare for your family celebration of Thanksgiving, think of ways to involve your toddler in the preparations.
♥ As you join hands on Thanksgiving, share with others the blessings your family has been given and give thanks throughout the year.

Celebrating Thanksgiving
Joining Hands in Thanksgiving

Today's Song
Gather 'Round
Sing to the tune of "Frère Jacques."
   Friends and family,
   Friends and family.
   Gather 'round,
   Gather 'round.
   We join hands together,
   We join hands together.
   At a meal, at a meal.
For more verses replace the last line:
When we pray, While we play, Thanking God.

Today in the Nursery
   We joined hands and thanked God in many ways for family, food, and friends. We played a game and we exercised while praising God.

Family Activity
♥ As you prepare for your family celebration of Thanksgiving, think of ways to involve your toddler in the preparations.
♥ As you join hands on Thanksgiving, share with others the blessings your family has been given and give thanks throughout the year.

We Get Ready for Jesus

"Then the angel said to her, 'Do not be afraid, Mary, for you have found favor with God. Behold, you will conceive in your womb and bear a son, and you shall name him Jesus. He will be great and will be called Son of the Most High....' "

Luke 1:30-32

Session Options and Materials
- ❑ God's special-gift activity
  - ✗ fabric-sculptured or other child-safe crèche
  - ✗ a box for the crèche and Christmas paper
- ❑ "Jesus Is Born" story
  - ✗ building blocks and any other toy building-materials available
- ❑ Nativity craft
- ❑ One set per child of the Mary, Joseph, and baby Jesus patterns (page 83) copied on stiff paper and cut out
  - ✗ crayons or nontoxic markers
  - ✗ magnetic strips for the back of the Nativity patterns
- ❑ "Help Us Get Ready" prayer
- ❑ "Away in a Manger" song
- ❑ "Who Was There?" cube toss
  - ✗ one empty half-gallon milk carton; one large jingle bell; Christmas cards of Mary, Joseph, baby Jesus, shepherds, animals, and an angel; clear contact paper
- ❑ Copied family note for each child

Dear Caregiver,

Advent is not only the season to prepare for Christmas when we remember Jesus' first coming to us but also a time to direct our hearts and minds to await the second coming of Jesus at the end of time. Advent is certainly a time for prayerful and joyful expectations. The toddlers will feel the excitement of all the preparations going on at home and all around them. In this session the toddlers will unwrap a gift that holds a crèche to symbolize the greatest gift God has given us, the gift of God's Son. Share the story of the birth of Jesus over and over again with the toddlers. The more practice the children have with this wonderful event, the easier it will be to celebrate the Good News of Christmas.

A Prayer for You

Lord, help me to be mindful that Advent is a time to direct my heart and mind to Jesus through prayer and your word. Help me to find peaceful moments during this busy holiday season to give thanks for all the blessings you give me. Touch the hearts of the toddlers as they hear the story of your son's birth and prepare for the celebration of Christmas. Amen.

Advent
We Get Ready for Jesus
Sing the "Hello Song" found on page 119.

Welcome

God's special gift
Before the session, fill a box with a soft-sculptured or other child-safe crèche and wrap the box with decorated Christmas paper. Gather the children around you and place the gift box in front of you. After the toddlers have tried to guess what is in the box, unwrap the gift to discover its contents. As you look at the pieces of the crèche , tell the children that God loves us so very much that God gave us a very special gift. That gift is Jesus.

Song
Away in a Manger
Add these actions to this familiar Christmas carol.

> Away in a manger,
> (*point far away*)
> No crib for a bed.
> (*shake head back and forth to say "No"*)
> The little Lord Jesus
> Lay down his sweet head.
> (*rest cheek on folded hands*)
> The stars in the heavens
> Looked down where he lay.
> (*look up above and point across the sky*)
> The little Lord Jesus
> Asleep on the hay.
> (*close eyes and rest cheek on folded hands*)

Prayer
Help Us Get Ready
Invite the children to sit near the crèche quietly. Remind the toddlers that God is with us all the time. Say the following prayer:

Dear God, help us get ready to celebrate the gift of your son Jesus. Let us think about Jesus as we share your love with our families! Amen.

Story

Jesus Is Born
Using the crèche, tell the story of the Nativity over and over again. Make a stable with the toddlers, using blocks or any other building materials you may have in the room. Allow the children to take turns manipulating the figures.

Mary and Joseph went to Bethlehem.
Joseph made a bed with straw and a blanket.
God watched over them.
Jesus was born that night.
Mary kept Jesus warm and cozy
The animals squealed with delight.
God's angel told the shepherds
The shepherds came to see baby Jesus asleep on the hay.

Craft
Nativity scene

Use the patterns provided to copy one set of characters on stiff paper or tag board for every toddler in the nursery. Cut the characters out ahead of time. Invite the toddlers to add color to each, using crayons or nontoxic markers. Have the toddlers help you put a piece of magnetic stripping on the back of each character. Send them home in a plastic or brown-paper bag so the children will have a daily reminder of the Nativity on their refrigerators.

Wrap-up

Who was there?

Prior to the session, make a cube using a milk carton as shown. A large jingle bell should be placed inside the cube before it is covered. On each face of the cube, glue a different Christmas card picture of the following: Mary, Joseph, baby Jesus, shepherd, animals, angel (or star). Cover the cube with clear contact paper.

Picture cube

Gather the children and roll the cube. Which ever side lands up, ask the children, "Who was there when Jesus was born?" If the side with Jesus lands up, help the children to say, "God gives us Jesus."

Sing the "Good-bye Song" or "Blessing Song" found on page 119.

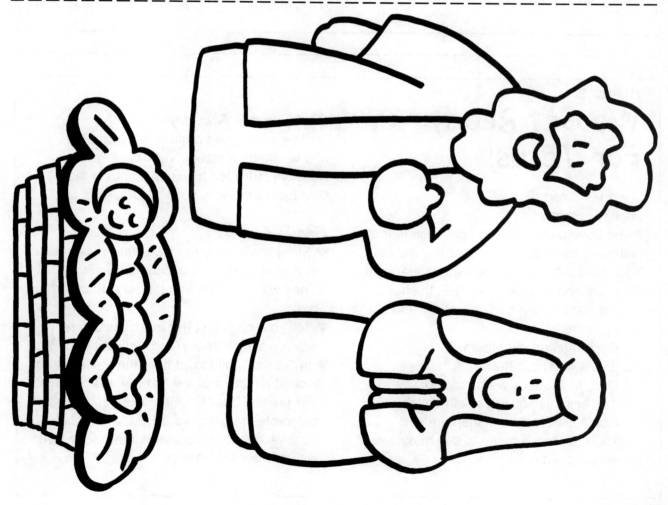

Advent
We Get Ready For Jesus!

Today's Story
Jesus Is Born

If you have a child-safe crèche, use it or a picture of the Nativity to help retell the story. Your child will never grow tired of hearing it.

Mary and Joseph went to Bethlehem.
Joseph made a bed with straw and a
   blanket.
God watched over them.
Jesus was born that night.
Mary kept Jesus warm and cozy
The animals squealed with delight.
God's angel told the shepherds
   The shepherds came to see baby Jesus
asleep on the hay.

Today in the Nursery
We unwrapped a gift. It was a crèche, and we made a stable. Then we heard the Nativity story. God loved us so much that God gave us a very special gift, Jesus.

Family Activity
♥ Store the magnet-backed Nativity figures in a contact-paper-covered coffee can. They will easily stick to the outside of the can.
♥ Tell your child that this is a special time when we think about God's gift of Jesus.
♥ Invite your child to sit near the crèche or to look at a picture of the Nativity as you say this prayer: Dear God, help us get ready to celebrate the gift of your Son, Jesus. Let us think about Jesus as we share your love with our families! Amen.

- -

Advent
We Get Ready For Jesus!

Today's Story
Jesus Is Born

If you have a child-safe crèche, use it or a picture of the Nativity to help retell the story. Your child will never grow tired of hearing it.

Mary and Joseph went to Bethlehem.
Joseph made a bed with straw and a
   blanket.
God watched over them.
Jesus was born that night.
Mary kept Jesus warm and cozy
The animals squealed with delight.
God's angel told the shepherds
   The shepherds came to see baby Jesus
asleep on the hay.

Today in the Nursery
We unwrapped a gift. It was a crèche, and we made a stable. Then we heard the Nativity story. God loved us so much that God gave us a very special gift, Jesus.

Family Activity
♥ Store the magnet-backed Nativity figures in a contact-paper-covered coffee can. They will easily stick to the outside of the can.
♥ Tell your child that this is a special time when we think about God's gift of Jesus.
♥ Invite your child to sit near the crèche or to look at a picture of the Nativity as you say this prayer: Dear God, help us get ready to celebrate the gift of your Son, Jesus. Let us think about Jesus as we share your love with our families! Amen.

Jesus Is Born!

"The angel said to them, 'Do not be afraid; for behold, I proclaim to you good news of great joy that will be for all the people. For today in the city of David a savior has been born for you who is Messiah and Lord. And this will be a sign for you: you will find an infant wrapped in swaddling clothes and lying in a manger....'"
Luke 2:10-12

Dear Caregiver,

Christmas is a time to celebrate the gift of Jesus and our experience of him in our lives today. Jesus is God's greatest gift to the world, and as we celebrate and share ourselves we become gifts of God's love to others. The toddlers experience the enjoyment of the Christmas season in many ways, including preparing for the celebration with decorations. Hanging decorations is an outward sign of the season. In this session the toddlers will continue to participate in the unfolding of this great story, and they will decorate the crèche with pretty paper-scraps, streamers, and ribbons as part of their rejoicing in the life of Jesus. Most importantly, we thank God for God's goodness and for sending us Jesus.

A Prayer for You

Joyously today, I celebrate with the toddlers the birth of Christ. You have given us a great gift in Jesus, a gift that has taught us to love and to share with others. Let us cover the world with your love and generosity. Amen.

Session Options and Materials

☐ "Who was there?" cube activity
  ✗ milk carton cube
  ✗ Christmas-card pictures of Mary, Joseph, baby Jesus, shepherds, animals, and an angel
☐ "Away in a Manger" action song
☐ "Baby Jesus Is Born" story
  ✗ wrist bells for each child, made ahead of time with 3-inch elastic and small jingle bells
☐ Stars and straw art
  ✗ art sheet copied from page 87 for each child
  ✗ star stickers
  ✗ straw or hay, or small pieces of yarn
  ✗ glue or paste
☐ "God's Gift" prayer
☐ Manger decorating
  ✗ variety of paper materials for decorating
  ✗ clear adhesive-tape
☐ Copied family note for each child

Celebrating Christmas
Jesus Is Born!
Sing the "Hello Song" found on page 119.

Welcome

Who was there?

Use the milk-carton cube from the Advent session. (If this is not available, prior to today's session see page 83, Session Eighteen, for directions on how to make this cube.) Gather the toddlers and ask them if they remember playing this game. The game is played by rolling the cube. Whichever side lands up, ask the children, "Who was there when Jesus was born?" If the side with Jesus lands up, help them to say, "God gave us Jesus."

Song
Away in a Manger
Add these actions to this familiar Christmas carol.

Away in a manger,
(*point far away*)
No crib for a bed,
(*shake head back and forth to say "No"*)
The little Lord Jesus
Lay down his sweet head.
(*rest cheek on folded hands*)
The stars in the heavens
Looked down where he lay.
(*look up above and point across the sky*)
The little Lord Jesus
Asleep on the hay.
(*close eyes and rest cheek on folded
  hands*)

Prayer
God's Great Gift
Invite the children to sit near the crèche quietly. Remind them that God is with us all the time. Say the following prayer:

You have given us Jesus to be our friend. This makes us so happy that today we celebrate this great gift. Thank you, God. Amen.

Story

Baby Jesus Is Born

Make a wrist bell for each child prior to the session by threading a jingle bell through the elastic. Cut the length of the elastic long enough to fit loosely around each child's wrist. Secure the loop by tying or sewing the ends of the elastic together .

Retell the story of Christ's birth using this song, sung to the tune of "The Farmer In the Dell," with the toddlers ringing their wrist bells.

Joseph finds a bed, Joseph finds a bed.
Refrain: Ring, ring, and sing with joy Jesus is born.
Verse 2: The baby is born
Verse 3: The animals make room
Verse 4: Mary keeps Him warm
Verse 5: The angel calls the shepherds
Verse 6: The shepherds come to see

Craft
Stars and straw

Copy one picture below for each child and provide star-stickers and straw for the toddlers to add to the sheet. Let the children decorate the sky with as many stickers as they wish to use. Ask each child to point the star that was special and showed where Jesus lay asleep. Make that one star stand out as special, by drawing rays around it, as shown. Glue pieces of straw to fill the bed for Jesus. Send home with the families for the children to use to retell the story.

Wrap-up

Decorate the manger

Set up the crèche in a special location of the room. Invite the toddlers to help you decorate the area. Provide a basket or box with a wide variety of paper scraps, streamers, and ribbons. Help the toddlers by attaching loops of tape to their selected decoration. They should hang the decoration wherever they wish. Throughout the decorating remind the children, "God gave us Jesus and we are so happy, we celebrate this today and always!"

Sing the "Good-bye Song" or "Blessing Song" found on page 119.

Celebrating Christmas
Jesus Is Born!

Today's Action Song
Away in a Manger
Add these actions to this familiar Christmas carol.

Away in a manger,
(*point far away*)
No crib for a bed,
(*shake head back and forth to say "No"*)
The little Lord Jesus
Lay down his sweet head.
(*rest cheek on folded hands*)
The stars in the heavens
Looked down where he lay.
(*look up above and point across the sky*)
The little Lord Jesus
Asleep on the hay.
(*close eyes and rest cheek on folded hands*)

Today in the Nursery
We sang a story about the day Jesus was born. We rang bells with joy because we were celebrating God's gift of Jesus, our friend.

Family Activity
♥ Hang your child's picture of the stable for all the family to see.
♥ As a family, share the story of Jesus' birth.
♥ Start Christmas traditions with your toddler that will continue over the years.
♥ During this season of gift giving, remember God's love is spread by sharing.

Celebrating Christmas
Jesus Is Born!

Today's Action Song
Away in a Manger
Add these actions to this familiar Christmas carol.

Away in a manger,
(*point far away*)
No crib for a bed,
(*shake head back and forth to say "No"*)
The little Lord Jesus
Lay down his sweet head.
(*rest cheek on folded hands*)
The stars in the heavens
Looked down where he lay.
(*look up above and point across the sky*)
The little Lord Jesus
Asleep on the hay.
(*close eyes and rest cheek on folded hands*)

Today in the Nursery
We sang a story about the day Jesus was born. We rang bells with joy because we were celebrating God's gift of Jesus, our friend.

Family Activity
♥ Hang your child's picture of the stable for all the family to see.
♥ As a family, share the story of Jesus' birth.
♥ Start Christmas traditions with your toddler that will continue over the years.
♥ During this season of gift giving, remember God's love is spread by sharing.

Jesus Loves Me!

"Beloved, let us love one another, because love is of God; everyone who loves is begotten by God and knows God. Whoever is without love does not know god, for God is love."
1 John 4:7-8

Session Options and Materials
- ❑ Searching for hearts activity
  - ✗ several hearts cut out of red, pink, and white construction paper
  - ✗ a large basket
  - ✗ lively music
- ❑ Valentine heart art
  - ✗ a heart shape cut out from stiff paper for each toddler
  - ✗ pre-cut ribbons and yarn
  - ✗ paper punch
  - ✗ stickers
- ❑ "If You're Loved" song
- ❑ "Jesus Loves Me" finger play
- ❑ "Hearts, Kisses, and Hugs" prayer
- ❑ "Parade of Hearts" march
- ❑ Copied family note for each child

Dear Caregiver,
Our capacity to love and be loved ultimately comes from God's love for us. That God loves us as Creator and Redeemer is best exemplified by Jesus' life and death. Love that mirrors God's steadfast and unconditional love makes love of self and neighbor possible. The toddler's most fundamental need is to be loved. It is the foundation of a positive self-concept. The toddlers will be delighted as you tell them that they are God's special creation and loved very much!

A Prayer for You
Dear God, thank you for surrounding me with your love and people who love me. Help me to be a mirror of your steadfast and unconditional love, to all the children I care for. Amen.

Welcoming the Little Ones

Valentine's Day
Jesus Loves Me!
Sing the "Hello Song" found on page 119.

Welcome

Searching for hearts

Cut out several hearts and place them around the room. Set out a large basket and play some lively music. As the toddlers are dropped off, tell them that today you will be celebrating Valentine's Day. Show them a heart and tell them that there are hearts hidden all around the room. Ask them to help you find the hearts and put them in the basket. After you have collected the hearts (you may want to play this game of hide-and-seek a couple of times), have the toddlers gather around the poster board on the floor. Ask the toddlers who loves them. Help the toddlers out by listing aunts, uncles, grandmas, grandpas, in addition to parents. Every time you hear a name mentioned, use a glue stick to attach a heart on the poster board, forming a large heart-shaped pattern. Say, "There are many people who love you! Valentine's Day is a day to celebrate love."

Song
If You're Loved and You Know It
Sing to the tune of "If You're Happy and You Know It."

> If you're loved and you know it,
> Clap your hands (*clap, clap*)
> If you're loved and you know it,
> Clap your hands (*clap, clap*)
> If your loved and you know it,
> Then your face will surely show it,
> (*point to a big smile*)
> If you're loved and you know it,
> Clap your hands! (*clap, clap*)

Explain to the toddlers that between verses you will say, "Who loves you?" Each time they may call out the names of people who love them.

Finger play

Jesus Loves Me

Jesus loves me ... (*hold the index finger up in the air, then point to self*)
When I walk. (*walk in place*)
Jesus loves me ... (*hold index finger up in the air, then point to self*)
When I jump. (*jump in place or carefully around the room*)
Jesus loves me ... (*hold index finger up in the air, then point to self*)
When I run. (*run in place*)
Jesus loves me ... (*hold index finger up in the air, then point to self*)
When I have fun. (*point to a very big smile*)
Jesus loves you ... (*hold index finger up in the air, then point to another friend*)
When you walk. (*walk in place*)
Jesus loves you. . . (*hold index finger up in the air, then point to another friend*)
When you jump. (*jump in place*)
Jesus loves you ... (*hold finger up in the air, then point to another friend*)
When you run. (*run in place*)
Jesus loves you ... (*hold finger up in the air, than point to another friend*)
When you have fun. (*point to a very big smile*)
Jesus loves everyone, (*point to each and every person in the room*)
He is God's loving son. (*hold finger straight up in the air*)

Prayer
Hearts, Kisses, and Hugs

Place a heart sticker on each toddler's clothes.

Thank you, Jesus, for all your love. We'll share your love by giving hearts, kisses. and hugs. Amen.

Craft

Valentine heart

Cut out a heart from lightweight tagboard for each toddler. Using a paper punch, punch the heart with random holes. Invite the toddlers to sew up the holes with the precut ribbons or colored yarn. Add stickers or other items. Put the toddlers' names on the back of their creations and encourage the toddlers to give their Valentines to people they love.

Valentine heart

Wrap-up

Parade of hearts

Give each toddler the heart that he/she made. Invite the toddlers to a Valentine's Day parade to celebrate God's love for them and their love for their families and others. Little ones can sit on the floor while the older toddlers are led joyfully around the room parading to upbeat children's music.

Sing the "Good-bye Song" or "Blessing Song" found on page 119.

Celebrating Valentine's Day
Jesus Loves Me!

Today's Prayer
Share this prayer with your toddler:

Thank you, Jesus, for all your love. We'll share your love by giving hearts, kisses, and hugs. Amen.

Today in the Nursery
We celebrated Jesus' love for us and our love for each other. We searched for hearts, made Valentines, and had a parade of hearts.

Family Activity
♥ Make heart-shape cookies with your toddler's help. Share the cookies and a glass of milk as you tell your child how much you love her/him.
♥ How to express and receive love is one of the most important things you can teach your child. Express your love in many ways every day with hugs, kisses, or by doing something special for someone.

Celebrating Valentine's Day
Jesus Loves Me!

Today's Prayer
Share this prayer with your toddler:

Thank you, Jesus, for all your love. We'll share your love by giving hearts, kisses, and hugs. Amen.

Today in the Nursery
We celebrated Jesus' love for us and our love for each other. We searched for hearts, made Valentines, and had a parade of hearts.

Family Activity
♥ Make heart-shape cookies with your toddler's help. Share the cookies and a glass of milk as you tell your child how much you love her/him.
♥ How to express and receive love is one of the most important things you can teach your child. Express your love in many ways every day with hugs, kisses, or by doing something special for someone.

Session Twenty-one — Lent
The Good Shepherd

"The gatekeeper opens it [the gate] for him, and the sheep hear his voice, as he calls his own sheep by name and leads them out. When he has driven out all his own, he walks ahead of them, and the sheep follow him, because they recognize his voice."
John 10:3-4

" 'I am the good shepherd, and I know mine and mine know me, just as the Father knows me and I know the Father; and I will lay down my life for the sheep.' "
John 10:14-15

Dear Caregiver,

A good shepherd took very good care of his sheep. There was nothing the sheep needed that wasn't provided. The shepherd watched over them, led them to food and water, and kept them safe from danger. A good shepherd knew his own and his own knew him. The toddlers will not completely understand the story of the Good Shepherd, but they will understand that God gives them people to love and care for them. The people who care for them do the same things that a shepherd does for his sheep. The toddlers are experiencing God's love through their caregiver's actions. Giving a hug, providing food, spending time with them, helping to search for something lost are just a few concrete examples. As toddlers grow, they will understand more and more about the Good Shepherd.

Session Options and Materials
❏ People-care-for-us activity
  ✗ bowl and spoon, pillow, blanket, jacket, container of adhesive bandages
❏ "Shepherd and Sheep" song
❏ "The Good Shepherd" story
❏ God's sheep craft
  ✗ one shepherd and sheep puppet-pattern per toddler cut from stiff paper, cotton balls, white glue, craft sticks (or gloves), markers, and scissors (for caregiver's use)
❏ "God Cares for Me" prayer
❏ Lost sheep game
❏ Copied family note for each child

A Prayer for You
Thank you, God, for knowing me by name, caring for me, giving me all that I need, and keeping me safe in your love. Thank you for these wonderful toddlers and help me to remember that each one is precious to you. Amen.

Lent
The Good Shepherd
Sing the "Hello Song" found on page 119.

Welcome

People care for us

Set the following objects around the room: bowl and spoon, pillow and blanket, a jacket, a container of Band-Aids. Sit down on the floor and ask the children, "Who helped you to get ready to come to church today?" Encourage them to tell you how they were helped. Invite them to look around the room and find a bowl and spoon. Ask them, "What are a bowl and spoon used for?" and "Who cares for you by cooking good things to eat?" Continue with the other three items in the same manner. Tell the toddlers that God also loves us very much and gives us people to care for us.

Song
Shepherd and Sheep

Using the patterns provided on the facing page, make shepherd and sheep puppets. Copy the patterns onto stiff paper and add a craft stick, or purchase an inexpensive pair of white work gloves and glue the pattern onto the palm of each glove. Introduce the sheep to the toddlers. Then introduce the shepherd. Tell the toddlers that people who take care of sheep are called shepherds. Invite the toddlers to move their hands in the same manner that you move the puppets as you sing this song to the tune of "Where is Thumkin?"

(*with the puppets hiding behind your back*)
Where's the sheep,
Where's the Shepherd?
Here she is, here he is.
(*bring the puppets out from behind your back*)
Hear the sheep say "baaaaa."
(*make the sheep move back and forth while the Shepherd is still*)
The Shepherd says, "I'll care for you
(*make the Shepherd move back and forth while the sheep is still*)
And keep you safe, keep you safe."

Story

The Good Shepherd

Begin by saying that Jesus told a story about God's love and care for us.

There was a Shepherd who had many sheep.
(*extend arm moving in a semi-circle to show many*)
The Shepherd cared for his sheep.
(*use hand as if to pat the sheep*)
One day he counted the sheep.
(*point to count sheep*)
One was missing!
(*hold up one finger*)
The Shepherd looked for his sheep.
(*put hand over brow to search*)
Then he found the sheep!
The Shepherd carried it back home.
(*circle arms to carry the sheep*)
Jesus tells us, God is like the Good Shepherd.
God watches over us (*raise arms, palms up*) and loves us (*use arm to hug self*).

Prayer
God Cares for Me
Invite the toddlers to sit quietly with folded hands as they repeat the following phrases.

Thank you, God, for watching over me with love and care both day and night. Amen.

Craft
God's sheep

Make a copy of the sheep pattern on stiff paper, then cut it out, one for each toddler. Give each child a sheep-shape and some cotton balls. Talk about how soft the cotton balls are. Spread white glue on the sheep and encourage the toddlers to put the cotton balls on the glue. Set the sheep aside to dry.

Wrap-up

Lost sheep

Ask the children what kind of sound the sheep makes. Encourage them to make the sound and to move around the room like a sheep. Invite one or two of the little sheep to hide and pretend to be lost. Say, "Oh, oh! Two of my sheep are lost. I must find them." Carefully move around the room looking for the lost sheep and then bring them back to the fold. Continue to do so until all the toddlers who want to hide have a chance to do so. End by telling them that the Good Shepherd cares for them.

Sing the "Good-bye Song" or "Blessing Song" found on page 119.

Lent
The Good Shepherd

Today in the Nursery

We heard a story about God's love and care for us called "The Good Shepherd." We made sheep and played the lost sheep game.

Family Activity

♥ Retell the story of the Good Shepherd. Then, folding your toddler's hands gently in yours, say this prayer: "Thank you, God, for watching over me with love and care both day and night."

Today's Story
The Good Shepherd

There was a Shepherd who had many sheep. (*extend arm moving in a semi-circle to show many*)
The Shepherd cared for his sheep. (*use hand as if to pat the sheep*)
One day he counted the sheep. (*point to count sheep*)
One was missing! (*hold up one finger*)
The Shepherd looked for his sheep. (*put hand over brow to search*)
Then he found the sheep!
The Shepherd carried it back home. (*circle arms to carry the sheep*)
Jesus tells us, God is like the Good Shepherd.
God watches over us (*raise arms, palms up*) and loves us (*use arm to hug self*).

Lent
The Good Shepherd

Today in the Nursery

We heard a story about God's love and care for us called "The Good Shepherd." We made sheep and played the lost sheep game.

Family Activity

♥ Retell the story of the Good Shepherd. Then, folding your toddler's hands gently in yours, say this prayer: "Thank you, God, for watching over me with love and care both day and night."

Today's Story
The Good Shepherd

There was a Shepherd who had many sheep. (*extend arm moving in a semi-circle to show many*)
The Shepherd cared for his sheep. (*use hand as if to pat the sheep*)
One day he counted the sheep. (*point to count sheep*)
One was missing! (*hold up one finger*)
The Shepherd looked for his sheep. (*put hand over brow to search*)
Then he found the sheep!
The Shepherd carried it back home. (*circle arms to carry the sheep*)
Jesus tells us, God is like the Good Shepherd.
God watches over us (*raise arms, palms up*) and loves us (*use arm to hug self*).

Session Twenty-two — Easter
Jesus Is Alive!

"Very early when the sun had risen, on the first day of the week, they came to the tomb. They were saying to one another, 'Who will roll back the stone for us from the entrance to the tomb?' When they looked up, they say that the stone had been rolled back; it was very large. On entering the tomb they saw a young man sitting on the right side, clothed in a white robe, and they were utterly amazed. He said to them, 'Do not be amazed! You seek Jesus of Nazareth, the crucified. He has been raised; he is not here. Behold the place where they laid him. But go and tell his disciples and Peter, "He is going before you to Galilee; there you will see him, as he told you." ' "

Mark 16:2-7

Dear Caregiver,

Easter is the high point of the Christian year, when we celebrate Christ's victory over sin and death, bringing new life. We also celebrate our part in the mystery of Christ's death and resurrection. The gift of Christ enables us to joyfully celebrate new life in our lives. When Mary Magdalene went to the tomb to anoint Jesus she was surprised at what she saw — divine life, where there had been none. The angel told her to go share this news with the disciples: "Jesus is alive." In this session the toddlers will look for new life and sing out in joy that Jesus is alive.

A Prayer for You

Lord, as we search for new life this spring, let me act as a messenger to these children, sharing the Good News that Jesus is alive in all of us. Amen.

Session Options and Materials
- ❑ "Which one?" activity
  - ✗ colored plastic eggs, at least one for each child
  - ✗ stickers of Jesus, at least one for each child
- ❑ "Jesus Is Alive" action rhyme
- ❑ "Chirping Birds" story
  - ✗ copied and colored story patterns (page 125)
- ❑ New-life viewer craft
  - ✗ paper-towel tubes, one for each child
  - ✗ crayons
  - ✗ curling ribbon
  - ✗ scissors for caregiver's use
- ❑ "New Life" prayer
- ❑ Hide-and-find game
  - ✗ basket
  - ✗ chenille Easter chicks (optional)
- ❑ Copied family note for each child

Celebrating Easter
Jesus Is Alive!

Sing the "Hello Song" found on page 119.

Welcome

Which one?

With the children sitting on the floor near you, place three plastic, colored egg-halves in front of you. In the sight of the children, place a sticker of Jesus under one of the eggs. Slide the three eggs around, changing their positions. Ask the toddlers, "Which one is Jesus under?" Invite a child to turn one over. Continue until they discover which one has the sticker under it. Play until the children tire of the game. The first few times the toddlers may need some help deciding which egg the sticker is under, but soon they will catch on how to play. While playing tell the toddlers that Jesus gives us new life. In the spring we discover new life all around.

Rhyme

Jesus Is Alive

In the spring …
The fluffy little bunny goes
Hop, hop, hop. (*hop in a circle*)
The little baby chicky says
(*in a low squatting position, say*)
"Peep, peep, peep."
The little child of God
Shouts with joy,
"Hooray, hooray,
(*raise arms up high with each shout*)
Jesus is alive!"

Prayer

New Life

Jesus,
Keep my eyes
(*point to eyes*)
And heart open
(*pat heart with hand*)
So I will always find you.
(*open arms in outward motion*)
Amen.

Story

Chirping Birds

(*Use the patterns on page 125 to retell this story about new life.*)

One spring morning, Adam woke up to the sounds of birds chirping. (Ask the children, "Do you hear the birds outside when you wake up?") He jumped out of bed and put on his play clothes. He wanted to know what was happening that the birds were making so much noise for. When he got outside, he tried to find where the chirping was coming from. He looked by the flowers growing in his mother's garden. But there were no birds. He found only fresh flowers that smelled so beautiful. ("Have you smelled flowers before?") He looked by his sandbox but saw only a bright-orange butterfly fluttering by. He heard the chirping again, so he followed the noise over to a big tree with lots of shiny new green leaves. ("Do the trees near your house have green leaves?") When he looked up, he saw a brown-and-orange bird sitting on the edge of a nest. From inside the nest Adam could hear the chirping of three hungry baby birds. Adam was so excited he ran inside the house to get his mother. She took him to the window so they could see the nest without upsetting the mother and her babies. As they looked out the window, Adam and his mother saw the tiny baby birds eating the worms their mother had brought for them. The chirping sounded liked a spring song.

Craft

New-life viewer

Use a paper-towel or toilet-paper tube to make this telescope-like viewer. Decorate the viewer by punching a few holes at one end of the tube. Thread short pieces of curling ribbon through the holes and tie into place. Curl the ribbons using a pair of scissors. Provide stickers and crayons for the toddlers to decorate their viewer. When each child who wants to make a viewer has done so, go to a window and look for signs of new life outside.

Wrap-up

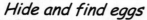

Hide and find eggs

Prior to the session, fill one plastic egg for each child with a sticker of Jesus and/or a chenille Easter chicky. Place the filled eggs in a basket. Walk around the room and with the help of the toddlers hide the filled eggs. After all the eggs are hidden, ask the children to search for the eggs and bring them back to you. Be alert to the children who may need help finding an egg. Keep hiding and finding the eggs. When the children leave to go home, give each child a plastic egg and a Jesus sticker. Invite the children to play "Which one?" at home with their families.

Sing the "Good-bye Song" or "Blessing Song" found on page 119.

Celebrating Easter
Jesus Is Alive!

Today's Rhyme
Jesus Is Alive

In the spring …
The fluffy little bunny goes
Hop, hop, hop. (*hop in a circle*)
The little baby chicky says
(*in a low squatting position, say*)
"Peep, peep, peep."
The little child of God
Shouts with joy,
"Hooray, hooray,
(*raise arms up high with each shout*)
Jesus is alive!"

Today in the Nursery

We celebrated Easter by looking for signs of new life in the spring animals using our New Life Viewer. We also hid eggs and searched the room for them.

Family Activity

♥ Use the egg and sticker that your child brought home to play a game of "Which one?" with your child. Hide the sticker under one of the egg halves. Then slide them around changing the position of the shells. Try to guess which one has the sticker under it.

♥ With your child search for other signs of new springtime life that will remind you of the joy of Easter morning throughout the season.

Celebrating Easter
Jesus Is Alive!

Today's Rhyme
Jesus Is Alive

In the spring …
The fluffy little bunny goes
Hop, hop, hop. (*hop in a circle*)
The little baby chicky says
(*in a low squatting position, say*)
"Peep, peep, peep."
The little child of God
Shouts with joy,
"Hooray, hooray,
(*raise arms up high with each shout*)
Jesus is alive!"

Today in the Nursery

We celebrated Easter by looking for signs of new life in the spring animals using our New Life Viewer. We also hid eggs and searched the room for them.

Family Activity

♥ Use the egg and sticker that your child brought home to play a game of "Which one?" with your child. Hide the sticker under one of the egg halves. Then slide them around changing the position of the shells. Try to guess which one has the sticker under it.

♥ With your child search for other signs of new springtime life that will remind you of the joy of Easter morning throughout the season.

Session Twenty-three — Celebrating Summer
God Is with Me!

"The Lord will guard your coming and going, both now and forever."
Psalms 121:8

Dear Caregiver,
Send the toddlers into the summer season with God at their side. We cannot see God, but we believe God is everywhere. A simple game of "peek-a-boo" is the beginning of helping toddlers discover God is everywhere. Hiding their eyes behind their hands helps toddlers to realize things exist even when we do not see the object. This session will give toddlers yet another opportunity to experience God's love all around them, wherever they are.

A Prayer for You
God, this has been a year full of excitement, learning, and laughter. Thank you for being at my side as I explored the world of your creation with these children. As we move into the summer season, continue to be at our sides in our play, work, and rest. Amen.

Session Options and Materials
❑ Peek-a-boo activity
   ✗ stacking blocks
❑ "I See You!" action rhyme
❑ Bubble echo movement
   ✗ bubbles and wand
❑ "God's Love" prayer
   ✗ hula hoop
❑ Summer-hat craft
   ✗ a paper bowl, tag-board square, and metal brad for each child
   ✗ crayons
   ✗ paste
   ✗ brightly colored tissue-paper
   ✗ embroidery floss (optional)
❑ Floating bubbles activity
   ✗ fan
   ✗ bubbles and wand
❑ Copied family note for each child

Celebrating Summer
God Is with Me!
Sing the "Hello Song" found on page 119.

Welcome

Peek-a-boo
   Build towers with the children using building blocks. Stack the blocks, then pretend to hide behind the tower. Peek around the side and say, "Peek-a-boo, I see you! Do you see me?" Invite the children to do the same. Lift the top block from the stack and peek between the blocks saying, "Peek-a-boo! Now do you see me?" As the play continues, talk about how God is always near, even though we do not see God.

Rhyme
I See You!
   One, two, (*use fingers to count*)
   I see you. (*point to someone*)
   Three, four, (*use additional fingers*)
   Not anymore. (*hide eyes behind hands*)
   Where did you go? (*keep eyes covered*)
   One, two, three, four, (*use fingers to count*)
   I'll just have to look some more.
   (*open and search for a child*)
   There you are!

Prayer
God's Love
Bless each child by placing a hula hoop around him or her and saying the following prayer.

   God, your love is all around [toddler's name]. Thank you for always being near. Amen.

Movement

Bubble echo
Read each line and encourage the toddlers to repeat the line back to you. As they are repeating it back to you, blow bubbles up in the air so they fall around the children.

   Bubbles floating in the air
   I can hardly feel that they are there.
   Watch and look! You will see!
   Bubbles floating down on me.
   In the air God's love is found.
   Just look and see it's all around!

   Challenge the toddlers to poke, to stomp, to clap, and to catch the bubbles. Some toddler will even enjoy trying to blow bubbles from the wand.

Craft
Summer hat

Before the children arrive, make each child a hat using a paper bowl for the base. Attach a square of tag board on the top, securing it with a metal brad as shown in the photo. Invite the toddlers to decorate their hats with crayons. For extra color, provide small pieces of brightly colored tissue-paper for the toddlers to paste to the hats. If you have children who will be leaving the nursery to move into a parish early-childhood program, you may want to make their hats into graduation hats by adding an embroidery floss tassel.

Summer hat

Wrap-up

Floating bubbles

Before the children arrive, set up a fan in the room completely out of any child's reach. Don't forget to check the dangling electrical cord.

While waiting for the parents to return, turn on the fan and blow bubbles in front of the fan. Invite the children to move through the floating bubbles trying to catch them with their hands. Remind the children God's love is all around them even if they cannot see it. God's love is everywhere.

Sing the "Good-bye Song" or "Blessing Song" found on page 119.

Celebrating Summer
God Is with Me!

Today's Rhyme
I See You!
One, two, (*use fingers to count*)
I see you. (*point to someone*)
Three, four, (*use additional fingers*)
Not anymore. (*hide eyes behind hands*)
Where did you go? (*keep eyes covered*)
One, two, three, four, (*use fingers to count*)
I'll just have to look some more.
(*open and search for a child*)
There you are!

Today in the Nursery
Playing peek-a-boo, we talked about how sometimes we cannot see something that really is there, like God. We also blew bubbles and made a summer hat.

Family Activity
♥ Hide objects for your toddler to find. Just because we can't see God does not mean God is not there.
♥ While with your child reinforce the concept that God is everywhere, in the smell of fresh flowers, in the sound of singing birds, and in each of us.
♥ Bless your child often with the sign of the cross to remind her/him God is always present.

Celebrating Summer
God Is with Me!

Today's Rhyme
I See You!
One, two, (*use fingers to count*)
I see you. (*point to someone*)
Three, four, (*use additional fingers*)
Not anymore. (*hide eyes behind hands*)
Where did you go? (*keep eyes covered*)
One, two, three, four, (*use fingers to count*)
I'll just have to look some more.
(*open and search for a child*)
There you are!

Today in the Nursery
Playing peek-a-boo, we talked about how sometimes we cannot see something that really is there, like God. We also blew bubbles and made a summer hat.

Family Activity
♥ Hide objects for your toddler to find. Just because we can't see God does not mean God is not there.
♥ While with your child reinforce the concept that God is everywhere, in the smell of fresh flowers, in the sound of singing birds, and in each of us.
♥ Bless your child often with the sign of the cross to remind her/him God is always present.

The ABCs of Connecting Church, Caregiver, Family, and Child

The following pages will help you organize your nursery in a manner that welcomes and informs all participants.

Check Lists, Policies, and Forms
✓ promotion check list
✓ opening check list
✓ closing checklist
✓ safety check list
✓ sign in/out sheet
✓ child information
✓ family welcome
✓ nursery policy sheet
✓ supply requisition
✓ injury report

Toddler Topics
☞ crying toddler tips
☞ diapering/toileting tips
☞ temper-tantrum tips
☞ snack tips

Caregiver Resources
✗ tunes for tots
✗ action songs
✗ movement activities
✗ needed item list

Promote Your Nursery

Be sure to spread the word to your parish about the good news of the nursery. Here are just a few ideas to help.

☞ **Use a bulletin board in a main hallway to:**
- Share pictures taken in the nursery
- Display artwork done by toddlers
- Introduce the nursery staff via pictures and quotes
- Exhibit parenting articles
- Announce family activity events
- Inform parishioners of upcoming parenting seminars
- Post days and times the nursery is open
- Distribute flyers about the nursery by having a nine-by-twelve-inch manila pocket file-folder marked "For You!"

☞ **Use weekly parish bulletin to offer short notes about:**
- Family life cartoons
- Book titles for families, parents, and toddlers
- Days and times the nursery is available
- Volunteer opportunities and name of contact person
- Recommended family activities
- Inspirational thoughts and quotes

☞ **Have an open house**
- An open house is an excellent way to inform parents and anyone else who is interested in the ministry.
- Schedule one or two a year during a time when the church attendance has been high (early fall for a harvest open-house, during Advent, or before Lent for a Mardi Gras open-house). Before or after Mass is usually the most convenient time for parishioners.
- If possible, have the entire nursery staff present so that parents and children have the opportunity to get acquainted.
- Plan one or two activities that the parents and children could sit down and do together if they choose (check out the craft ideas in sessions for simple ideas).
- Serve a toddler treat such as animal crackers and apple juice.
- Talk briefly about the ministry of the nursery and answer any questions. Supply information sheets to go home.
- The goal is to make everyone feel welcome and as comfortable and confident as possible.

Opening the Nursery Check List

✓ Make the nursery welcoming
- Place a bright, cheerful easel outside the doorway to welcome families and post names of the day's nursery staff, perhaps under their pictures.
- Illuminate the room with natural lighting, if available, and overhead lighting if needed.
- Arrange furniture and toys in a manner that invites children to play. To prevent toddlers from wanting to run, divide the wide-open spaces with furniture and/or activities. Set toys and books out to involve the toddlers when they first arrive.
- Room temperature is at a proper setting.

✓ Make the nursery safe
- Do a safety check of the room and the equipment (see page 108).
- Be sure there are enough staff and volunteers to provide proper supervision for the opening of the nursery. A safe recommended ratio is one caregiver or volunteer to every three toddlers.

✓ Make the nursery practical
- Check to insure completed "child information forms" are in the room for easy reference.
- Place the "sign-in sheet" and blank "child-information forms" with pens near the door for parents.
- Check on materials needed for the day's activities:
    - ✗ supplies for craft and activities;
    - ✗ snack, cups, napkins, paper towels, and handi-wipes;
    - ✗ diapers, paper sheets to line changing surface, baby wipes, covered basket, or sealable plastic bags for diaper disposal

Once this check list is complete you will be prepared to give your full attention to the children and families as they arrive.

 # Closing the Nursery Check List

- Clean up any spills or spots that require special attention.
- Check room for any personal articles left by children or families.
- Materials and furniture are returned to proper place.
- Broken equipment and toys are reported or removed as appropriate.
- Requisition form is filled in for next session's needs.
- Trash and soiled diapers are disposed of properly.
- Thermostat is set at proper setting.
- Lights are turned out.

Check List for Safety

Safety is a primary consideration in caring for toddlers. Here are a few tips that will assist in childproofing the nursery. Be sure to observe from the toddler's view.

Adjust:
- dangling electrical or mini-blind cords,
- furniture and table-coverings that may be pulled down

Check that:
- electrical plugs are covered
- door knobs are covered
- decals are on windows and sliding glass doors

Remove:
- broken or damaged toys or equipment
- small pieces that might be inhaled or stuck in ears or nose
- items that may be inhaled and swell when dampened

Avoid:
- glitter
- balloons
- plants

Sign In and Out

Today's nursery leaders are: _____

_____

_____

Parent or guardian: Please print your child's name and sign name upon arrival. Upon departure please sign OUT.

CHILD'S NAME	Parent/Guardian SIGN IN	Parent/Guardian SIGN OUT
_____	_____	_____
_____	_____	_____
_____	_____	_____
_____	_____	_____
_____	_____	_____
_____	_____	_____
_____	_____	_____
_____	_____	_____
_____	_____	_____
_____	_____	_____

This page can be reproduced on a photocopier.

Child Information Sheet

God made me, and my family has named me _____
(child's name)

I live with _____
(list parents/guardians, siblings)

My favorite pet is named_____

I mostly like to play (check all that apply):
__alone   __with adults   __ with other children

My favorite activities at home are:_____
_____
_____

My known allergies are (please list all allergies, especially food allergies): _____

What I especially want you to know about me is: _____
_____
_____

The only people who may pick me up from the nursery are:
_____
_____

In case of an emergency, contact:
_____
(name and phone number)

Parent/guardian's signature:_____

Parent/guardian's phone number: Days_____
Evenings _____

Here's the Nursery Scoop!

We are very happy to welcome you and your child to the nursery. Your family will find this a comfortable and secure place to leave your child or grandchild. We know that toddlers are always learning and that the seeds of faith are already growing in your little one's heart. With the help of our nursery leaders, the toddlers learn more about God's love for them through simple songs, finger plays, movement activities, and stories. We are very enthusiastic about making the nursery a special and fun place to visit each week.

Where: The nursery is located _____

When: The nursery opens at _____ and closes at _____ .

Please stop in to visit us whenever the nursery is open or call the nursery coordinator for more information.

Who: The nursery is coordinated by: _____ .

The nursery is staffed by: _____

_____

Phone(s): _____ .

If you would be interested in occasionally volunteering in the nursery, please contact the nursery coordinator.

Why: Your child will learn that the parish nursery is a safe and happy place to be. This experience is the beginning of your toddler's understanding that he or she belongs to a parish family who knows and cares about him or her. We are anxious to provide a loving environment for your toddler and to support your family as you grow in faith together!

Welcome to the Nursery!

We want you and your family to feel comfortable in the nursery. Here is some useful information that will help you to become more familiar with us.

Ages
- The nursery is open to toddlers ages twelve months through thirty-six months.

Sign-in
- The sign-in sheet will be posted near the door. The parent/guardian who brings in the child (or children) should sign in him or her (individually if more than one) to the nursery.
- If your child is new to the nursery, please take a moment to fill in a short *Child Information Form*, also posted near the door.
- Print your child's name on the name tag provided and place it on his/her back. We request that parents label all diaper bags, sipper cups, etc., with the child's name. Masking tape is available.

Dropping Off and Picking Up
- If you arrive before the nursery leader, please stay with your child until the leader arrives. Children are not to be left alone.
- Please do not send older children to drop off or pick up your child. If an adult other than the parent/guardian has permission to pick up the child, please inform the nursery staff.
- Be sure to sign out your child when you pick him/her up.
- Please pick up your child as soon as possible following Mass or other parish activity.

Diaper-Bag Needs
- Diapers
- Plastic bottle or cup
- A change of clothes

Illness
- Please do not bring your child to the nursery if she/he is not feeling well.

Nursery leaders may not give medication to any child.

Thank you for your family's cooperation. We want all of our toddlers to be happy, healthy, and safe!

Supply Requisition
(Please indicate by circling)

Housekeeping

paper towels	supply low	supply depleted
diaper wipes	supply low	supply depleted
diapers	supply low	supply depleted
tissues	supply low	supply depleted
other _____	supply low	supply depleted

Arts and Crafts

glue or paste	supply low	supply depleted
tape	supply low	supply depleted
other _____	supply low	supply depleted

Snacks

juice	supply low	supply depleted
cups	supply low	supply depleted
napkins	supply low	supply depleted
other _____	supply low	supply depleted

Nursery Forms

child information	supply low	supply depleted
volunteer sign up	supply low	supply depleted
sign in/out	supply low	supply depleted
injury	supply low	supply depleted

Special Requests: _____

_____

_____

_____

_____

Submitted by: _____ Date: _____

Injury Report

Name of child injured: _____

Type of injury: _____

Date of injury: _____ Time of injury: _____

Details of incident (include location, witnesses, etc.): _____
_____
_____
_____
_____
_____

Treatment provided: _____
_____
_____
_____
_____

Name of Parent/Guardian notified: _____

Completed by: _____
Date: _____

Toddler Topics
Settling a Crying Toddler

Reasons for crying may vary from child to child. It is easier to settle the crying child when you understand what has caused the emotion:

- ♥ separation
- ♥ injury
- ♥ frustration
- ♥ exhaustion

Assure the child of the parent's return.

Be positive, patient, and do not scold.

Comfort and sit with the crying child where she/he can view other children at play.

Distract the child with a conversation about him- or herself, family members, or animals they may have at home. Use the Child Information Sheet so you can talk with the child about family members and pets by name.

Engage in a different or new activity:
- ✔ take a short walk away from the room
- ✔ look out a window and talk about what can be seen
- ✔ read a book
- ✔ make a picture for parents

Remember: patience, patience, patience.

Diapering/Toileting Tips

For diapering the toddler, it is suggested that:

○ The diaper-changing surface be lined with a disposable paper sheet and/or the surface wiped down with a disinfectant.

> *Caution: Ideally, disinfectants work best for eliminating germs on changing tables but are toxic to toddlers. If using, do not use near children and keep out of their reach at all times.*

○ The child should never be left unattended during the diapering process.

○ Disposable baby wipes are used to cleanse the child during diapering, wiping from front to back.

○ The soiled diaper, wipe, and paper liner are disposed of in a covered trash can or sealed in a plastic bag until proper disposal is possible.

○ The caregiver's hands are washed thoroughly after the diapering and disposal of diaper-changing materials .

For toileting the toddler that is being potty trained, it is suggested that:

○ Close communication is kept between the parents and the caregivers, including:

- what phrase the child uses to communicate the need,
- how often the child should be prompted, and
- how much help the child needs using the bathroom.

○ The caregiver's and child's hands should be washed before and after toileting.

○ If an "accident" happens use a matter-of-fact attitude to:

- try toileting again,
- change the toddler as needed and place clothes in sealed plastic bag, and
- reassure the child that he or she is still learning and next time will be more successful.

○ Do not scold.

To prevent the spread of infectious diseases, it is important that sanitary precautions be considered each time diapering or toileting takes place in the nursery.

Practical Thoughts About Temper Tantrums

Consider the possible causes for these emotional outbursts:

✓ expressing feelings of hunger, exhaustion, over-stimulation, boredom, independence, frustration,

✓ announcing "I am here!", or

✓ losing control of emotions.

Avoid the occasions for tantrums by:

✓ Anticipating situations before they arise.

> Provide duplicate toys to help keep children from fighting over a favorite toy.

✓ Organize wait time.

> Sing songs, say rhymes, or make a game of the time between activities.

✓ Warn the toddlers of upcoming transitions or changes to take place.

✓ Try to provide a consistent routine while being flexible:

> Toddlers like the security of knowing what is going to happen next. At the same time, they want to be able to keep a good thing going.

✓ Allow two choices of activity if possible, but remember that too many choices can be just as frustrating as not having any choice (having a few activities going on at once allows the toddler to choose which to participate in).

✓ Be patient and listen carefully when trying to understand the child's developing language or speech. This means getting down to his or her level, eye-to-eye.

Each child and situation can be very unique and so will the manner in which you deal with tantrums.

Depending on the situation, you might try:

• redirecting or distracting the child's attention to a new activity,

• ignoring the behavior and letting it burn itself out,

• helping the child put his/her frustrations into words,

• offering snacks to the hungry toddler, or

• providing a rest area for the tired toddler.

But always:

✓ Protect the child and those around from being harmed. If needed, move the child to a safe area for an opportunity to "cool off" or until the tantrum has "burned itself out." At no time should any child be left alone.

✓ Be a model of God's forgiving, tender, loving, patient, and kind care.

Super Tips for Serving Snacks

Toddler hospitality requires a handy snack at all times. No matter what time of day it is, toddlers always seem to need a little something to munch on. Here are a few suggestions:

- ✓ Check the Child Information Form for any known allergies.
- ✓ Keep the snacks simple so they can be pulled out and served in a minute. Easy snacks for toddlers include: animal crackers, Cheerios (or any other low-sugar cereal), graham or soda crackers, and toddler-bite-size pieces of fruit. Apple juice is always a hit to drink.
- ✓ Ask parents to bring a sipper cup with their child's name marked on it. (Masking tape and a marker should be made available to those who need to label theirs.) Keep small paper cups handy for those who are new or forget theirs.
- ✓ Wash toddlers' hands before snacks are served. (Use handi-wipes if a sink is not available.)
- ✓ Invite the children to a designated snack-spot.

When the toddlers are sitting, serve the snack. The snack-spot could be on the floor around a vinyl tablecloth, around child-size tables, or at a low table with chairs.

Serve the snack whenever the children ask or seem to need it (or when you need it). In the nursery, don't try to keep snack at a specific time. No matter how you plan it, the time will probably vary from week to week.

Encourage the toddlers who are having snacks to put their hands together as you say this short prayer of thanksgiving:

> *Thank you, God, for the snack we eat.*
> *Sharing with friends is really a treat. Amen.*

Bon Appetit!

Caregiver Resources
Tunes for Nursery Tots

Hello Song
Sing to the tune of "Frère Jacques"
Come to play, come to play,
Nursery friends, nursery friends.
Nursery friends it's Sunday!
We have come to sing and say,
God is good, God is good.

Hello Friends
Sing to the tune of "Here We Go 'Round the Mulberry Bush"
Hello friends, I'm glad you're here,
Glad you're here, glad you're here.
Hello friends, I'm glad you're here,
We will have a great time!

Picking-Up Song
Sing to the tune of "London Bridge"
It's time to put the toys away,
Toys away, toys away.
It's time to put the toys away,
So we can play another day.

Snack Time
Sing to the tune of "Skip to My Lou"
Snack snack snack for you
Snack snack snack for you
Snack snack snack for you.
God bless our yummy food.

Taking-Turn Song
Sing to the tune of "Mary Had a Little Lamb"
Kelly had her turn today,
Turn today, turn today.
Kelly had her turn today,
Now it's Terry's turn.

Good-bye Song
Sing to the tune of "Good Night Ladies"
Bye-bye friends, bye-bye friends,
Bye-bye friends,
God bless you on your way.
(or, God keep you safe and sound.)

Blessing Song
Sing to the tune of "This Old Man"
God bless you, God bless me,
God bless everyone you see.
With a prayer for you
And a prayer for me,
God bless you and God bless me.

Action Songs and Activities for Tots

Toddlers' endless energy requires plenty of opportunities to move around. Action songs and activities allow them to further develop their coordination and balance.

Action Songs

Ring Around the Rosie

Ring around the rosie,
Pocket full of posies.
Ashes, ashes,
We all fall down.

Hold hands with the group and walk around in a circle. The group falls to the floor on the last line.

London Bridge

London Bridge is falling down,
Falling down, falling down.
London Bridge is falling down,
My fair lady (or gentleman).

Two people make a bridge with their hands and the others walk under the bridge. The "bridgers" capture the person under their hands for the last line of the song.

Head, Shoulders, Knees, and Toes

Head, shoulders, knees and toes,
knees and toes.
Head, shoulders, knees and toes,
knees and toes.
Eyes and ears and mouth and nose.
Head, shoulders, knees and toes,
knees and toes.

Point to each body part as mentioned.

The More We Get Together

Traditional German Tune

The more we get together,
Together, together.
The more we get together
The happier we'll be.
For your friends
Are my friends,
And my friends
Are your friends;
The more we get together,
The happier we'll be.

Row, Row, Row Your Boat

Row, row, row your boat,
Gently down the stream.
Merrily, merrily,
Merrily, merrily,
Life is but a dream.

Sit on the floor with a toddler, facing each other hold hands and rock back and forth.

If You're Happy and You Know It

If you're happy and you know it,
clap your hands. (*clap, clap*)
If you're happy and you know it,
Clap your hands. (*clap, clap*)
If you're happy and you know it,
Then you're face will surely show it.
If you're happy and you know it,
Clap your hands. (*clap, clap*)
Other actions and verses:
  • tired, give a yawn
  • sad, wipe your eyes
  • hungry, pat your tummy
  • grumpy, make a face

Johnny Hammers

Johnny hammers with one hammer,
One hammer, one hammer.
Johnny hammers with one hammer all day long.
(*tap one fist on floor*)

Other actions and verses:
• two hammers (*tap two fists*)
• three hammers (*tap two fists and one foot*)
• four hammers (*tap two fists and two feet*)
• five hammers (*tap two fists, two feet, and head*)
Final verse:
Johnny's very tired now, tired now, tired now.
Johnny's very tired now, he lies down. (*lie down*)

Movement Activities

Parachute Play

Gather around the edges of the parachute. Grasp the edges, lift, and shake the parachute.

- Place soft toys or balls on the parachute and bounce them about in the same manner, shaking the edges of the parachute and trying to keep the toys in the chute.
- Place toys under the parachute and invite the children to guess what it is that is hiding under the chute.

Blanket Rides

Have toddlers sit on a blanket while holding onto the edges. A caregiver pulls the blanket by one of the corners, giving the children a ride around the room.

Stop-and-Go Dancing

Play some marching or dancing music. Start and stop the music, encouraging the toddlers to dance or march when the music is playing and stop when the music is not.

Toddlers on Parade

Give the toddlers streamers of fabric or paper and invite them to parade around the room. Play some lively music in the background.

Follow the Leader

A "leader" gives simple commands for the toddlers to follow. A few suggestions would be:

- point to your elbow
- bend and touch your knees
- clap your hands
- touch your head
- jump up high

Select commands that most of the group can handle. As the children get used to this game, the older toddlers may be ready to act as a leader and give the commands.

Obstacle Course

Set up an obstacle course for the children to move through using obstacles as follows:

- chair to climb over
- beam to walk on
- rope to jump over
- pillows to crawl over
- sleeping bag or mat to tumble on
- hoops to jump through or in
- boxes to crawl through

For the safety of the children, have a caregiver act as a spotter at the different obstacles.

Blow Bubbles

Blow bubbles for the toddlers to chase. Encourage the toddlers to poke, stomp, clap, and blow the bubbles.

Items to Gather For Nursery Fun

Collect for activities

___ juice-can lids
___ wrapping paper
___ cardboard cartons and boxes
___ toilet- or other paper-tubes
___ flat and fitted bed sheets
___ vinyl tablecloths
___ small towels
___ wash clothes
___ sponges
___ milk cartons of various sizes
___ Christmas cards
___ magazines
___ water squirt-bottles
___ plastic pitcher
___ plastic bowls
___ watering can
___ gift boxes with lids
___ shirts for paint smocks
___ dish pans or basins
___ jelly-roll pan
___ sleeping bag
___ plastic serving trays
___ sandpaper squares
___ wide yellow ribbon
___ Styrofoam meat trays
___ large pillows
___ ribbon scraps
___ magazines with pictures
___ yarn
___ Easter grass
___ straw or hay
___ basket
___ canvas bag

Purchase for activities

___ picture of Jesus with little children
___ stickers of Jesus
___ brightly colored cellophane gift-wrap
___ **Good Night Moon** book by Margaret Wise Brown
___ soft-sculptured or other child-safe crèche
___ hula hoop

Caregiver necessities

___ scissors
___ hole punch
___ permanent markers
___ clear adhesive-tape
___ masking tape
___ nametags
___ pens

Toys and books

___ picture books
___ fabric books
___ board books
___ puzzles (three to eight pieces)
___ push- and pull- toys
___ building blocks (plastic, cardboard, or wood)
___ sorting toys
___ nesting toys
___ stacking toys
___ parachute
___ sandbox toys
___ balls

Basics

___ paste
___ glue
___ construction paper
___ colorful tissue paper
___ wrapping paper
___ colored chalk
___ bubbles and wands
___ variety of stickers
___ contact paper
___ cotton balls
___ foil
___ plastic wrap
___ non-toxic washable crayons and markers
___ paper plates
___ craft sticks
___ tag or poster board
___ adhesive-backed magnetic strips
___ string
___ finger paint
___ shaving cream
___ coffee filters
___ food coloring
___ newspaper

Snack supplies

___ small paper cups
___ wet wipes
___ paper towels
___ napkins

Reproduce these flannel-board patterns and use with the story on page 14.

1

2

3

4

Reproduce these fish on a photocopier and cut apart for use with Session 11, page 55.

Reproduce these patterns on a photocopier and cut apart for use with Session 22, page 98.

Our Sunday Visitor...
Your Source for Discovering the Riches of the Catholic Faith

Our Sunday Visitor has an extensive line of materials for young children, teens, and adults. Our books, Bibles, booklets, CD-ROMs, audios, and videos are available in bookstores worldwide.

To receive a FREE full-line catalog or for more information, call **Our Sunday Visitor** at **1-800-348-2440**. Or write, **Our Sunday Visitor** / 200 Noll Plaza / Huntington, IN 46750.

Please send me:__ A catalog
Please send me materials on:
 __ Apologetics and catechetics   __ Reference works
 __ Prayer books   __ Heritage and the saints
 __ The family   __ The parish

Name_____

Address_____Apt._____

City_____State ____Zip_____

Telephone (   ) _____

A73BBABP

Please send a friend:__ A catalog
Please send a friend materials on:
 __ Apologetics and catechetics   __ Reference works
 __ Prayer books   __ Heritage and the saints
 __ The family   __ The parish

Name_____

Address_____Apt._____

City_____State ____Zip_____

Telephone (   ) _____

A73BBABP

Our Sunday Visitor
200 Noll Plaza
Huntington, IN 46750
1-800-348-2440
OSVSALES@AOL.COM

Your Source for Discovering the Riches of the Catholic Faith